LESSONS FROM
THE NAVY

LESSONS FROM THE NAVY

How to Earn Trust, Lead Teams, and Achieve Organizational Excellence

MARK BROUKER

ROWMAN & LITTLKEFIELD
Lanham • Boulder • New York • London

Although the author and publisher have made every effort to ensure that the information in this book was correct at press time, the author and publisher do not assume and hereby disclaim any liability to any party for any loss, damage, or disruption caused by errors or omissions, whether such errors or omissions result from negligence, accident, or any other cause.

Some names and identifying details have been changed to protect the privacy of individuals.

ROWMAN & LITTLEFIELD
An imprint of The Rowman & Littlefield Publishing Group, Inc.
4501 Forbes Blvd., Ste. 200
Lanham, MD 20706
www.rowman.com

Distributed by NATIONAL BOOK NETWORK

British Library Cataloguing in Publication Information available

Library of Congress Cataloging-in-Publication Data available

ISBN: 978-1-5381-3786-4 (cloth)
ISBN: 978-1-5381-3787-1 (electronic)

Library of Congress Control Number: 2020942256

♾ ™ The paper used in this publication meets the minimum requirements of American National Standard for Information Sciences—Permanence of Paper for Printed Library Materials, ANSI/NISO Z39.48–1992

For my wife, Kris, and children,
Shayna, Jacob, and Katherine.

Also to my dad, Paul Brouker,
and mom, Marlene Brouker.

CONTENTS

Introduction   1

1. *Insights*   7
2. *The Power of the Leadership Phenomenon*   23
3. *Interactions: Opportunities to Earn Trust*   37
4. *Know Your Staff*   55
5. *Be Visible*   75
6. *Respect*   93
7. *Don't Ignore Good or Poor Performance*   113
8. *Optimism*   137
9. *Continuously Learn the Art of Leadership*   163
10. *Leading in a Crisis*   167

Conclusion   177

Acknowledgments   181

Appendix: Recommended Reading   185

Notes   193
Bibliography   207
Index   213
About the Author   221

INTRODUCTION

People don't care how much you know until they know how much you care.

—Theodore Roosevelt

When I began this project a few years ago, I never put much thought into its title. However, *Lessons from the Navy* is perfect—the lessons I learned about leadership indeed came from my thirty years of service in the Navy. While the Navy taught me many lessons, the primary one was that effective leadership is not about command and control but about compassion and caring. Another lesson I learned is that everyone craves being led by an effective leader—people very much want their boss to be a great leader.

After transitioning from the Navy a few years ago, I started a leadership consulting company named Brouker Leadership Solutions (www.broukerleadershipsolutions.com). I'm forever grateful to the Navy for the opportunities to lead and the wisdom gained from my service. I now have time to dig much deeper to help understand why some leaders succeed while others fail.

In my travels since starting my company, I've seen professionals from a variety of areas—sports, health care, sales, banking, insurance, manufacturing, engineering, academia, and the military, to name a few—who, due to their proficiency as an individual contributor, were promoted to leadership positions. However, while these leaders appeared ready, willing and able to lead, in many cases they ended up leading teams that failed outright, woefully underperformed, or at the very least never came close to reaching full potential. This happened a lot, and I wanted to know why. As it turned out, the primary reason was that these new leaders didn't fully understand what it took to succeed in their new role. In my experience, observations, study, and research over the past thirty-five years, I've concluded that the key ingredient to effective leadership is caring for your people, and these struggling leaders did not make this task a priority. This is not to say that these leaders were uncaring individuals. However, their focus, attention, and energy were invested too heavily in other areas of the business and not in developing relationships with their employees. In other words, I've seen struggling leaders, for example, spend inordinate amounts of time focusing on results rather than *their* vitally important role in *achieving* those results.

The goal for every organization is mission accomplishment. Leaders who have a good working relationship with their employees build more trust up and down the chain of command. These leaders will create teams that accomplish the mission much more easily—with less drama, less turnover, and lower costs in labor and material, among other metrics—compared with teams that lack trust.

How does a leader earn trust? Leaders, researchers, and thought leaders generally agree that there are three essential ingredients. The first is technical competence. People are more likely to trust a leader whom they believe has the technical know-how and experience to make good decisions. The second is consistency. A leader must do what they say they will do, follow through on commitments, and keep their promises. (As a side note, I've learned to be very scrupulous about making promises—the more broken promises, the more trust that is at risk.) The last ingredient to earning trust is showing care and compassion. Leaders need to build relationships with their team members and show that they care for their teams' well-being. Competency, consistency, and caring—all three are important ingredients to earning trust. However, while competency and consistency are certainly important, neither is as vital to earning trust as showing care and compassion. As such, this task is the focus of my book.

Leading with care and compassion is an extremely powerful concept. I've seen leaders successfully lead teams in areas where the leader was not proficient in the technical aspect of the work. For example, I've seen Navy non-commissioned officers[1] whose expertise was aircraft maintenance successfully lead medical teams. While these leaders were certainly not rendering medical care to patients—they weren't proficient in this area—they *were* building strong relationships with their team members who *did* provide that care. What these leaders exceled in was their ability listen, show empathy, and make sure every sailor was able to feel engaged, fulfilled, supported, and recognized. These leaders were successful despite lacking technical competence because they focused their efforts on their unique role in achieving the results—they focused on behaviors that conveyed their concern for the sailor's well-being. In the end, they led with care and compassion.

The power of leading with care and compassion is not a new concept. In fact, it's been around for centuries. While the technologies that humans have created over the past two millennia have changed significantly, the very human dimension of leadership has not. History teaches us that all great leaders have touched the souls of their followers by showing them that they care for their well-being—this magical connection inspires people to overcome the greatest of calamities and to face any danger. What did the great ancient philosophers have to say about the importance of leading with care and respect?

Aristotle stated that by showing concern for others, leaders would inspire respect instead of fear.[2] Plato wrote that the leader's duty was to take care of the needs of the followers over their own needs.[3] Xenophon (a pupil of Socrates and an ancient Greek historian, philosopher, and soldier) stated that everything a leader does must demonstrate to his subordinates that they constantly think of *their* welfare and work for *their* benefit.[4]

It would appear that Alexander the Great heeded the advice of these ancient thought leaders. From 334 BC to 323 BC—one hundred years after Xenophon and mere decades after Plato and Aristotle—Alexander subdued the largest tract of the earth's surface ever to be conquered by a single individual. How did he lead? He treated his soldiers with respect and cared for their well-being. For example, he granted home leave to all the men who had been married before the fighting began, he always made sure his men were well fed and well rested, he showed great concern for the wounded, and he listened patiently as his soldiers recounted their exploits.[5] Alexander the Great cared for his soldiers, and that care was reciprocated with superior effort.

A mere 150 years ago, a great leader emerged who saved the hope for a system of free government for countless generations. Abraham Lincoln, viewed by most historians as the greatest leader the United States has ever known, led in a time of tremendous uncertainty. During America's bloodiest war, Abraham Lincoln built and led an army that was inspired to go beyond what anyone thought possible. Lincoln treated all people, including those who were opposed to him, with the utmost respect. He took time out of his incredibly busy schedule to hear what people had to say, created friendships that paid enormous dividends over the course of the war, and spent time circulating among his troops.[6] Lincoln's overall leadership style was a case study of what the ancient philosophers championed: earn the trust of your team members by showing care and respect toward them.

In 1959, Viktor Frankl, an Austrian psychiatrist as well as a Holocaust survivor who between 1942 and 1945 labored in four different camps (including Auschwitz), published his epic book, *Man's Search for Meaning*. The book has sold more than ten million copies in twenty-four languages and is one of the most influential books ever written. In it, Frankl wrote, "The immediate influence of behavior is always more effective than that of words."[7] Therefore, with respect to leadership, the fastest way to earn more trust is through the leader's behaviors, not words. More specifically, behaviors that convey care and compassion— the way the leader treats others and the regard they have for others— expedites the trust-building process.

For leaders today, what does care and compassion look like? It's a leader who—in spite of an extremely busy schedule—goes out of their way to build relationships with *all* team members. It's a leader who makes themselves available, listens empathetically, and knows a little about each team member. It's a leader who gets people excited about the work, helps them understand the importance of the work, and fosters pride in their work. In the end, these are leaders who people not only *want* to follow but also *love* to follow.

My choice of the word *love* is a deliberate one, and accurate. Fascinating research has recently shown that when a team member feels care and compassion from their leader, profound changes occur at the neurotransmitter level within their body. This intriguing topic will be discussed in much more detail later in this book. The bottom line for now is that it would appear that Theodore Roosevelt's words of wisdom spoken over one hundred years ago ("People don't care how much you know until they know how much you care") are indeed true.

While the bulk of my practical experience is based on military leadership structure, I've learned that leading with care and compassion can earn enormous trust in any industry or organization. Since my transition from the military, my passion has led me to work with diverse organizations in twenty-one countries—investment banks, insurance companies, academic institutions, civilian medical teams, professional sports organizations, and both Fortune 500 companies and small businesses from a variety of industries. The research I've gathered, concepts presented, and techniques suggested can be universally applied in any setting.

My passion is to enlighten leaders to understand not only the enormous power of leadership but also, more specifically, the power of caring. I wrote this book to inspire leaders to make the small investment needed—through the use of practical and easily applied leadership behaviors that are presented in the following chapters—to transform them into the great leader that is within them.

1

INSIGHTS

> Trust is the most critical element of successful leadership. It provides the fundamental bedrock for the relationship between the leader and the led.
>
> —Christopher Kolenda, *Leadership: The Warrior's Art*

As I drove west from Newport, Rhode Island, to San Diego, California, my trepidation increased with each passing mile. I couldn't ignore the mounting butterflies in my stomach. I had a healthy fear of the unknown, and there was no shortage of unknowns ahead.

I had left a well-paying, steady job as a retail pharmacist in Washington, D.C., and voluntarily joined the Navy as an active duty pharmacy officer. It was a change that created a lot of unanswered questions in my life. Had I made the right career decision? Would I like the Navy? What would the job be like? More importantly, did I have what it takes to be a good officer? A good leader? All these unknowns made the Navy a big mystery. One of the few certainties I did have was my annual salary, which had decreased from $30k to $15k. With that certainty came another concern: How would I adjust to the drastic pay cut?

My exposure to the Navy up to that point in my life was through intriguing stories told by my dad. Although he had only been in the Navy for a couple years, it clearly had a major impact on his life. Dad loved his time in the Navy.

Enlisting after high school in 1949, my dad's brief time in the Navy had him on board the heavy cruiser USS *Rochester*, battling massive storms in the North Atlantic, firing five-inch guns at empty ships, and palling around with some of the most interesting characters one could imagine. After my dad left the Navy in 1951 after just two years, he spent the next thirty-seven years working as a blue-collar employee at the local General Electric factory in my hometown of Pittsfield, Massachusetts. However, if you ever had an opportunity to have coffee with my dad, you'd swear he'd spent thirty-seven years in the Navy and only two years at General Electric!

My dad's love of the Navy and his stories of adventure no doubt impacted me in a number of ways. I felt his deep love of country and profound patriotism. I felt his pride in being part of a noble cause. He loved being in the Navy because he was part of something bigger than himself. His Navy stories painted a picture of close friendships and an "all for one and one for all" mentality. The camaraderie among his shipmates was palpable and conveyed deep relationships that were clearly not replicated during his many years at General Electric. His Navy pals were a band of brothers. His stories inspired me, and, even as a young boy, I secretly desired to have the same experience.

One name that was often woven into my dad's Navy tales was Chief Tandy[1]—my dad's first boss in the Navy and a man whom he grew to greatly respect. My dad's face would light up whenever he mentioned this name. Said with obvious affection, my dad's standard line was "Chief Tandy cared for me like a son. I would've done anything for him. I loved that man!" Outside of his own immediate family, my dad never mentioned anyone with the same emotional outpouring as he did when he spoke of this mysterious man, Chief Tandy. It was clear to me that Chief Tandy had cared for my dad deeply and that my dad had an enormous amount of respect for him. And yes, my dad worked very hard for him. As it turned out, Chief Tandy provided my first insight into leadership.

Even as a boy, and later as a teenager, there was a spark of interest within me to understand how, by simply caring for my dad, Chief Tandy had earned my dad's love, respect, admiration, and trust. Over time, this burgeoning curiosity turned into a burning passion that ignited a lifelong journey to understand the secret of how to lead others, the power of caring, and the power of trust.

My Navy adventure began when I reported to Navy Base, Newport, Rhode Island, for Officer Indoctrination School (basic training for staff

CO. 191 - C.L. TANDY G.M.C.   CO. CMDR.
U.S. NAVAL TRAINING CENTER GREAT LAKES ILL. 16, AUG. 1949.

In this slightly damaged photo, Chief Tandy is front and center. My father, Paul Brouker, is in the back row, second from the left.

corps officers) in May 1983. Within twenty-four hours of reporting, I knew that I had made the right decision. After five years of college and three years working in the civilian sector, for the first time in my life I was part of something truly bigger than myself. I and about a hundred other newly minted naval officers quickly forged close friendships. We were all small cogs in a complex organization that was tasked to defend our country's freedom. I was very excited and beaming with pride to be part of it. I had found my calling in the Navy.

After that basic training, I took a few days to visit my family in Western Massachusetts before I started my drive cross country to my first duty station in San Diego. During that short visit in Pittsfield, I was given some sage advice from my cousin, Steve Brouker. Steve was a chief in the Navy and, at that time, had served in the Navy for about ten years. Steve was a natural leader and loved the Navy, maybe even more than my dad did. Steve counseled me well on the importance of chiefs—how their leadership and ability to maintain good order and discipline within the enlisted ranks was vital to the success of the Navy. More importantly, Steve repeatedly told me that the most important thing I needed to do—really, the *only* thing I needed to do—was take care of my sailors. That's how you *really* earn their trust.

Steve's advice was always delivered in a unique and colorful way; he made swearing an art.

"Take f—n' care of 'em!" he bellowed to me the last time we spoke before I started my drive west. "And don't forget . . . the chiefs are the f—n' backbone of the Navy!"

Parsing the colorful language, I couldn't help but note that Steve's advice was eerily similar to my dad's stories about Chief Tandy. Driving away and heading west on I-90, I thought that maybe there *was* something to this "caring" stuff.

In July 1983, I reported to my first duty station, Naval Hospital San Diego, as a pharmacy officer. Outfitted in a brand-new, smartly creased summer white uniform, polished white shoes, and a sparkling brass belt buckle, I was full of enthusiasm and hope, or "piss and vinegar," as was the more common vernacular in the Navy. Despite the confidence that came naturally after completion of basic training, the broader question that belies the success of any military officer gnawed at me: Do I have what it takes to be a good officer? A good leader?

As an officer escorted me through the pharmacy areas within Naval Hospital San Diego that morning, I kept hearing noise and commotion from behind one door in particular. My escort simply ignored the pandemonium. However, each time we passed the door, my concern heightened.

Why was I concerned? Unfortunately, while I had only worked a couple of years in pharmacies, they were all chaotic, noisy, and extremely busy ones. Phones constantly ringing, staff noisily talking over one another with patients and physicians, and the incessant grind of automated pill counting machines meant that there was rarely any break in the clatter. Up to that point in my career, I found that morale was often low and smiles were rare in the very few pharmacies that I had worked in.

My concern was that the noise coming from behind the door sounded eerily familiar, and I quietly prayed that whatever was happening behind it had nothing to do with where I'd be working. Whatever it was, I wanted nothing to do with it.

To my chagrin, we stopped at that door. My escort turned to me and casually said, "Here it is: our last stop. The outpatient pharmacy area. This is where you'll be working. We fill a ton of prescriptions! It's a real zoo—you'll see!"

Alas, my greatest fear was realized.

He opened the door, and we were hit with a cacophony of noise and activity—phones ringing; people scurrying past one another; hurried discussions about medications, patients, doctors, and a host of other topics. It all combined into what appeared to me as absolute chaos.

I tried desperately to appear unflustered by it all. However, I'm sure everyone saw me as a typical young ensign looking like the proverbial deer in the headlights.[2] I walked around meeting an endless array of people, trying in vain to commit at least one or two names to memory.

Among the swirl of introductions that day, I was eventually introduced to one person who stood out among the others. I immediately sensed that this person commanded respect. It was palpable. It was clear that he had the trust of *everyone* in that room.

He was Chief Smock, and he had one of the most difficult jobs in the pharmacy department and arguably the entire hospital. He was the leading chief petty officer of the Outpatient Pharmacy Division, and he was responsible for keeping the seventy-five or so staff members on task with the seemingly endless process of accurately filling thousands of prescriptions each and every day. While that's a good technical description of his job, I saw it as simply being in charge of utter chaos. However, despite the pandemonium, I noticed something odd. Despite the noise, chaos, and tumult, the staff were smiling and appeared to be actually *enjoying* themselves.

In the middle of this maelstrom, Chief Smock calmly greeted me with a kind smile and warm handshake. He undoubtedly saw through my pitiful attempt to appear unmoved by the overwhelming flurry of noise and activity.

Although I didn't ask it, he sensed my bewilderment and desire for an answer to the obvious question: How did these people so readily endure the chaos, the monotony of the work, the constant interruptions, day in and day out, and still appear to enjoy the work? He took this opportunity to impart some wisdom to this young officer.

Chief Smock locked eyes on me and with a confident smile remarked, "Sir, this leadership thing's pretty simple. Take care of your sailors and they'll take care of you . . . and they'll trust ya."

There it was again: care and trust. A pattern was emerging.

Chief Tandy, cousin Steve, Chief Smock—they all seemed to think that the secret to leading was trust, and the key to trust was taking care of your people. This couldn't be mere coincidence; there had to be something to it. It certainly piqued my interest. Could the key to leading others be as straightforward as earning their trust by caring?

Twenty-five years after that encounter with Chief Smock, my wife, Kris, and I found ourselves once again driving westward across the United States. This move west was a bit more complicated than the one we had embarked on as newlyweds in 1983. Back then, the two of us were heading west with a couple hundred pounds of old furniture and junk. However, in 2008, Kris and I were joined by three children, two cats, one dog, and *twenty thousand pounds* of old furniture and junk.

I had been selected as commanding officer (or CO) of Naval Hospital Bremerton in Bremerton, Washington,[3] and when we arrived I would assume command of that hospital.[4] I knew this was an incredible opportunity; as commanding officer I would be able to put into action at the C-suite level within a complex organization a leadership philosophy that I grew to passionately embrace, supported by tried and tested techniques that I had refined over the years. What was that philosophy? Earn trust by proving to your subordinates that you care.

This philosophy was forged by a quarter century of insights gained by observing other leaders of *all* ranks, intense study, and hands-on experience, the latter being by far the most impactful part of my learning.

Leadership Lesson

Take care of your people, and they'll take care of you.

During my years in the Navy leading numerous teams on Navy installations around the country, overseas, and onboard ships, I had run the gauntlet, and that gave me firsthand knowledge of which leadership techniques worked . . . and which didn't. That wealth of experience was augmented by formal and informal study. Both while getting my master in business administration and attending the Naval War College, I analyzed, studied, researched, and authored numerous case studies on effective and ineffective leadership. I read hundreds of books on leadership, team building, and trust while in school and on my own. I attended any and all leadership development classes offered through the Navy—sometimes twice. I weaseled my way into leadership development classes sponsored at local colleges. I sought out all learning opportunities. The more I learned about leadership, the more voracious my appetite to learn grew. I found the topic to be both mystifying and fascinating, and still do to this day.

In the end, as I was preparing to assume command, I came to the same conclusion about leadership as Chief Tandy, cousin Steve, and Chief Smock: To maximize your effectiveness as a leader, you must earn trust by caring for your people. However, I also realized something that, while of vital importance, was not referenced in books, articles, or curriculum, nor discussed among prominent leaders. Amazingly, most leaders either are unaware of or take for granted this important fact: leaders intrinsically generate more fear than trust. By nature of the role of leadership, it is inevitable that, along with the title of "leader," there comes a level of intimidation. Leaders can be intimidating because they wield enormous control over at least half the waking hours of their employees. Why is this of vital importance? Leaders who do not proactively address this natural state of affairs will lead underperforming teams. They will constantly wonder why their employees remain silent when their opinions are needed, why change is agonizingly slow and always full of drama, and why good people leave. Employees who are intimidated aren't focused on doing better—they're focused on not making a mistake.

In my seminars I often tell of the conversation I had with my son, Jake, when he started his Navy career as a twenty-two-year-old newly minted ensign. I wanted to warn him of this pitfall.

"Jake, remember, you're intimidating. You're an officer, and you have a lot of control over the sailors who work for you. You're in a position of authority. By default, you're intimidating, and you need to proactively work to break down that intimidation. You want your sailors to tell you what you *need* to hear, not what you *want* to hear."

I remember Jake looking at me with an incredulous expression.

"Dad," he said, "I'm just tryin' to figure out how to do my job. I'm an ensign. Who am I gonna intimidate?"

His answer is one that most leaders would utter. Most leaders do not realize that they are intimidating or take it for granted. Worse yet, others intentionally use their rank or position to intimidate employees, which, of course, creates fear. Regardless, they do not actively work to decrease their level of intimidation, and so they lose out on significant opportunities.

About halfway through my Navy career, I began to formulate my leadership philosophy in earnest. I began to appreciate the power of caring, the need to drive out fear and earn trust. I saw the benefits of being an approachable leader. Around that time, I moved to a new leadership job, and on my second day on the job my new boss scheduled our first one-on-one meeting. During that meeting I remember him asking me what my plans were for the first couple of months on the job.

Reflecting back on all the insights gained during my naval career up to that point, I knew exactly what my goal was going to be: to show everyone who worked for me that I deeply cared for their well-being, because I did, and to do it quickly. I was the boss. The new leader. The people whom I would lead didn't know me. The natural state of affairs on day one would generally default to a culture of fear. My goal was to ensure that they understood the value of their work and truly enjoyed their work. I was acutely aware that the sooner they knew I cared for

---

Leadership Lesson

Because all leaders control important aspects of people's lives (i.e., whether they remain employed), leaders need to be aware that their role comes with some level of intimidation.

them, and cared for them deeply, the sooner they'd begin to trust me. Only when they felt comfortable around me and had confidence and faith in me as a leader would we be able to successfully navigate the unknown, inevitable, and innumerable changes, crises, challenges, and landmines that laid in our path.

I proudly and confidently explained this to my new boss. My confidence wilted when he stared at me for what seemed like hours before he finally spoke.

Incredulously, with a look of both absolute disdain and grave concern, he asked, "That's it? That's your plan?"

I don't recall much of the conversation after that, but I obviously recovered from it enough to keep my job. Like many leaders, he didn't appreciate that the natural state when a new boss takes over defaults to fear. I wanted to reverse that. Despite his obvious misgivings, I stuck to my plan, and we enjoyed abundant success over the ensuing three years.

I employed that same philosophy in all subsequent jobs, and it always proved successful. I certainly used it during my command tour at Naval Hospital Bremerton. What happened over those next three years in command had a profound impact on me. I witnessed firsthand how caring for my team members created intense trust and how that transformed a complex organization of fifteen hundred diverse individuals into a high-functioning team. I was very fortunate to have been surrounded by many extremely talented people at Naval Hospital Bremerton. In large part because of their dedication, loyalty, and support, Naval Hospital Bremerton performed at an extremely high level during my three years in command. We enjoyed abundant success. As an example, among the ten Navy hospitals in the same region—a region titled Navy Medicine West that spanned the West Coast to the Indian Ocean—Naval Hospital Bremerton was the only hospital to exceed its workload goals; we had the highest dental readiness,[5] the top-rated logistic program, the top-rated limited duty program,[6] and the highest third-party collection rate.[7] Our command climate surveys were always well above the Navy-wide average,[8] and we were the first Navy hospital worldwide to achieve a 100 percent score on an urgent and important series of data quality metrics. Of all Navy hospitals worldwide, our Integrated Disability Evaluation System was rated number one,[9] as was our force protection plan.[10] Naval Hospital Bremerton was the only family physician teaching hospital in the Navy with a 100 percent board certification pass rate,[11,12] and our hospital was named one of Washington state's top hospitals for "best care." Our success culminated in the command earning a prestigious Meritorious Unit Commendation along with numerous regional and national awards, including awards for community service, training, patient safety, limited duty processing, energy conservation, and active duty member retention.

What was my role in this success story? I understood from day one that to create a high-performing team, I needed to lead the effort and set the example to proactively build strong relationships with my team members. I needed to drive out the fear that naturally comes with positions of authority. I consistently used vital leadership techniques to ensure everyone in my command knew that I genuinely cared for them. Over a period of time, these efforts resulted in improved trust up and down the chain of command. This culture of trust was well documented in the numerous command climate surveys that the members of my command routinely completed. As a result, when I asked for opinions on any issue, I was told the truth and not what they thought I would want to hear. Because I was better informed, decision making was optimized, necessary change was made with minimal drama, and the crises that we faced were dealt with effectively. What was the key to our success? I had confidence in them, and they had confidence in me.

After my command tour, I was promoted to serve as the chief of staff, Navy Medicine West in San Diego, California, which was my last tour of duty in the Navy. As chief of staff, I was the chief operating officer for a region of ten hospitals that employed fifteen thousand people and spanned the West Coast to the Indian Ocean. We provided health care for eight hundred thousand patients within that vast region.

One of the most gratifying aspects of my job was providing executive coaching for the ten commanding officers in the region. These men and women worked extremely hard, and I was honored to help them navigate the numerous challenges that came with command. We talked about a wide variety of topics, from issues festering within their commands to wrestling with the work-life-balance conundrum. We also talked about leadership. While I knew how busy they were, I encouraged each of them to prioritize relationship building and make it part of their daily routine.

Of course, some heeded that advice more than others. While all commanding officers in our region had successful command tours, those who proactively worked to build strong relationships enjoyed smoother sailing: their commands were more proficient in dealing with change and crisis management, had superior key performance indicators, and all in all had more enjoyable command tours. The reason for these successes was their focus on caring for their people, which built trust up and down the chain of command.

After my transition from the Navy, I've witnessed firsthand the importance of earning trust in leadership throughout the private sector. I started a leadership consultancy company and, with the luxury of additional time, I was able to study leadership with increased vigor. More importantly, I've traveled around the world speaking with thousands of leaders from diverse cultures and all levels of leadership within corporations, nonprofits, academic institutions, sports organizations, and, of course, military units. What additional insights have I gained from these fascinating conversations?

As in the military, leaders in the private sector generally don't understand that they intrinsically generate more fear than trust. Further, most leaders don't make relationship building a top priority. Sometimes it's not a priority at all. The numbers tell the story. According to Gallup, only about a third of managers in the United States are engaged (employees perceive them to care for their well-being), while the rest are disengaged (employees perceive that they don't care). Worldwide, the numbers are much worse: only 13 percent of managers are engaged. Disengaged managers lead disengaged teams, resulting in lower productivity and lower overall team performance.[13]

Second—and this is what's a bit astonishing—while leaders don't make relationship building a priority, they've personally experienced the profound impact that a caring leader had on them as they climbed the corporate ladder. At the beginning of my leadership development seminars, I ask participants to think about the truly great leaders that they've either worked for or played for—a boss, a coach, a professor—who impacted them in a positive way and truly inspired them to go above and beyond. I then ask them to recall what this leader did to garner such a maximal effort. The words "care" and "trust" are *always* uttered and, when they are, *all* participants *always* enthusiastically agree. Like my dad describing Chief Tandy, these men and women describe these caring leaders with an unusual emotional outpouring. These leaders are considered great because they cared, and their caring was reciprocated with trust and, more importantly, higher team performance.

So, on the one hand, leaders understand through firsthand experience what motivated them as they climbed the corporate ladder: caring leaders whom they trusted. On the other hand, and quite paradoxically, these same leaders are not practicing the relationship-building behaviors required to build that trust. Consequently, it remains a grossly underutilized practice. Why is this the case? It's an important question; we need to understand why leaders aren't making relationship building a priority. Here are three reasons:

1. While it is certainly important that the leader be both competent and honest in order to earn trust, the caring part of earning that trust is severely underappreciated. The simple, yet extremely powerful, practice of building relationships with your people has been diluted, and maybe washed away, in the flood of research, data, articles, and books on the topic of leadership. The idea of taking care of your people has been overlooked and overwhelmed by the ubiquity of leadership development content.

2. Building trust is prioritized behind other, less important, prerogatives. Faced with endless meetings and conference calls, 24/7 technology-enabled connectivity, and leading smaller teams with increased work, even the most resilient leader can become overwhelmed. A recent Deloitte survey of twenty-five hundred executives in ninety-four countries found that overwhelmed leaders and employees are a global concern with implications not only for those leaders but for their organizations as well.[14] Putting out fires and tending to other urgent matters is given priority over building the team's trust.

3. Leaders don't know how to appropriately build relationships with their team members. Some may not know how to appropriately show acts of caring. Behaviors that convey a caring style are not included in the standard curricula of most business schools or in most leadership development seminars offered

through corporations, nonprofits, academic institutions, and sports organizations.

This book provides solutions to each of these impediments. While busy leaders may be cognizant of the vital importance of earning trust through relationship building and acts of caring, the truth is that most are not making it a priority. Leaders don't appreciate the sheer power of their leadership. Others have misconceptions about the characteristics of a successful leader. Sadly, some of these leaders actually intend to lead by fear. These individuals do not appreciate that fear stifles creativity and productivity. In this environment, employees will be less likely to speak up when they have a process improvement suggestion for fear of criticism. Worse, mistakes will more likely be covered up. These leaders grossly underestimate how their behaviors impact team trust, overall team culture, and ultimately team performance. When leaders discover the power of caring (which this book will reveal), readers will be more inspired to prioritize relationship building in their daily routine.

A subordinate's trust in their leader is *the* most important factor in the success of any organization. The team members' confidence in the leader provides the fundamental bedrock for the relationship between the leader and the followers.

Are there specific behaviors that a leader can easily employ to show that they care that earn enormous trust? In fact, there are. Through experience, research, study, and observation, I've found six critical behaviors—all practical, all easy to use, and all proven to improve team performance—that a leader can employ to show that they care for their subordinates. The profound impact that each of these has on trust will be uniquely conveyed through personal stories, current and historic case studies, and solid research. It is important for leaders to understand that to

---

Leadership Lesson

To optimize your effectiveness as a leader, *all* six behaviors discussed in this book need to be employed.

optimize their effectiveness, *all* six behaviors discussed in the subsequent chapters must be employed. Further, while these six behaviors are powerful, the book will also help the reader fully understand that *all* the leader's behaviors—day by day, hour by hour, minute by minute, second by second—impact trust.

Is trust lacking in the workplace? Absolutely. However, it doesn't have to be this way. Considering that only one in eight leaders worldwide appears to care for their workers, there is enormous untapped potential to create much more trust in the workplace. If even half the leaders make this a priority, imagine how the world could be different. If schools; universities; banks; manufacturers; retailers; hospitals; churches; charitable organizations that serve the public by supporting the arts, funding medical research, or championing human rights causes; or a host of other organizations were led by trusted leaders, imagine the possibilities.

Who is able to employ these simple yet powerful behaviors? Anyone. While these behaviors are powerful, they're not complex. Employing them takes discipline and time. While the investment is minimal, the return on that investment is enormous.

As my thirty-year Navy career came to a close, I realized that the insights I gained from Chief Tandy, cousin Steve, and Chief Smock all those years before had proven to be true. In addition, the insights gained from all that I had experienced, all that I had observed, and all that I had studied over that thirty-year span (but especially during my command and chief of staff tours) led me to conclude that the secret to effective leadership is trust, and the key to earning trust is taking care of your people. When led by a leader who cares, employees will trust their leader, work harder for them, and find more joy and satisfaction in their work. Care, trust, and effort are inexorably interlocked and proportional. The more caring, the more trust, the greater the effort.

Leadership Lesson

A subordinate's trust in their leader is *the* most important factor in the success of any organization.

KEY POINTS

1. Take care of your people, and they'll take care of you.
2. Because all leaders control important aspects of people's lives (i.e., whether they remain employed), leaders need to be aware that their role comes with some level of intimidation.
3. To optimize your effectiveness as a leader, *all* six behaviors discussed in this book need to be employed.
4. A subordinate's trust in their leader is *the* most important factor in the success of any organization.

2

THE POWER OF THE LEADERSHIP PHENOMENON

Phenomenon: An unusual, significant, or unaccountable fact or occurrence; a marvel.

—Webster's Dictionary

How powerful is leadership? Can we describe leadership as a "phenomenon"? Is it powerful enough to fall into that exclusive category?

Over the many years that I've been practicing, studying, and discussing leadership with other leaders from around the world, one of my most fascinating discoveries is that the vast majority of leaders do not appreciate the power of their leadership. They do not understand the enormous influence they wield as leaders. Why is this important? When leaders fully appreciate this power and the enormous influence they have over others, they're stirred to take the necessary steps to improve their ability to lead—to inspire others and get things done. It's important for all leaders to reset, to take a step back, to understand and appreciate the enormous influence they wield. That's what we're going to do in this chapter.

From 2003 to 2006, I worked at the Bureau of Naval Personnel and led a small team of highly talented individuals whose job it was to assign officers to Navy commands around the globe.[1] The Navy's title for this human resource job is "detailer." The typical officer in the Navy moves to a new tour of duty about every three years. My team was responsible for ensuring three thousand naval officers had jobs that were career enhancing, challenging, and overall suitable for themselves and their families. As an example, we were sometimes tasked with convincing a naval officer, and their family, that a move from Hawaii to Iceland was in their best interest. Needless to say, it was a fascinating job.

Over the three years that I held that position, I had literally thousands of conversations with officers as we balanced the needs and desires of individual officers and their families with the needs of the Navy. The needs of the Navy were inordinately high—this was the height of our wars in Iraq and Afghanistan. We were stretched thin in many areas, and we needed all hands on deck. My team worked hard to keep as many of our top-performing officers in the Navy as possible.

Through that process, I would sometimes have multiple conversations with the same officer over a period of weeks. In a perfect world, these conversations ultimately resulted in me "writing orders" for the officer to detach from their current command and report to another command. However, as you can imagine, the process (by its nature) is complex. Sometimes this was not the outcome of our conversations. It must be remembered that the United States Armed Forces is an all-volunteer force. A viable option for any officer who had completed their obligated service was to tell me, or any detailer, that they're not interested in another tour; they're getting out of the Navy. This, of course, happened.

Through the thousands of conversations I had with officers over those three years, I came to better understand why an officer would elect to leave the Navy. Often these motives were quite predictable: perhaps they found an excellent job opportunity in the civilian sector or a spouse or child did not want to move. Interestingly, deploying into harm's way—which was very common during those years—was *never* mentioned as a reason for leaving the Navy. There was, however, one particular factor that played a significant role in an officer's decision to stay or leave that I found alarming: it was leadership—specifically, whether the officer had been led by a good or poor leader.

The conversations I had with officers who had been supervised by leaders they admired and respected were in stark contrast to those I had with officers who answered to leaders they neither admired nor respected. Thankfully, the vast majority of my conversations fell into the former group—they were well led. These officers were generally excited about the Navy and their future role in it. That is not to say that they all stayed in the Navy. However, those who did elect to move on generally had well-thought-out reasons for the decision.

Regarding the latter group (those who were not well led), I could sometimes convince an officer to stay in the Navy and take orders to another assignment if they had only worked for *one* poor leader. However, I could *never* convince *any* officer to stay in the Navy if they had worked for two poor leaders in a relatively short period of time, despite offering these officers excellent jobs in beautiful parts of the world, like Spain or Hawaii. These poor leaders led strictly by command and control. They tended to micromanage and had a "my way or the highway" and "do it because I said so" leadership philosophy. While a certain degree of anxiety is healthy—it inspires individuals to overcome obstacles and helps them achieve greater potential—these leaders created excessive anxiety and fear. Working under these conditions over a period of time resulted in their officers becoming angry, dispirited, and bitter. They were burned out and wanted nothing more to do with the Navy. Consequently, and tragically, these officers got out of the Navy.

Many of these officers were truly talented, had exceptional service reputations, and had earned excellent fitness reports.[2] Our country needed these officers' leadership and unique skills to help fight and win our nation's wars. The Navy was losing excellent officers at a crucial time in our country's history due to something seemingly within our control: poor behaviors by those in positions of leadership. Again, while the vast majority of officers with whom I spoke were well led, this discovery was very disturbing.

Another, more revealing, pattern I found in the officers we could not retain was the raw emotion they exuded as they described working for these poor leaders. I will never forget their anger as they told their stories. Their voices revealed anxiety, sleeplessness, and outright trauma as a result of working for these leaders. I had similar conversations with officers who experienced truly horrific events during deployments to unsafe, austere areas of Afghanistan and Iraq. However, amazingly, I had more conversations with officers traumatized by poor leadership than I had with officers traumatized by the ravages of war. What I learned from this experience is that the maxim "people don't leave bad jobs, they leave bad leaders" is true.

My good friend Bob, a Navy buddy of many years, is an excellent

> ## Leadership Lesson
>
> People don't leave bad jobs; they leave bad leaders.

example of the level of anxiety perpetrated by a poor leader. When Bob returned from a difficult twelve-month deployment to Afghanistan a few years ago, we met for coffee in Washington, D.C. Bob told me that the most horrifying time he'd endured in Afghanistan was a period when he and his unit were receiving random mortar fire from the enemy. No one knew where the next mortar would land. The potential for death and trauma was random.

We met many more times for coffee over the ensuing months. I learned that Bob wisely sought out mental health treatment and received the care he needed. The first few months after his return, I couldn't help but notice his hands would sometimes shake. With his ongoing mental health treatment and the healing that comes with time, about nine months or so after his return, the shaking disappeared. Bob was visibly back to himself.

About two years after his return from deployment, Bob and I met again for coffee. Bob's demeanor had changed significantly. He looked tired and worn, and his hands were occasionally shaking once again. During the course of our conversation, I asked him if something had triggered his memories of the mortar attack.

Smiling, he said, "Hell no. I've got a new boss whose driving us all nuts." Getting more wound up as he spoke, he continued with increasing emotion, "The boss is a micromanager, always looking over our shoulders, checking up on us. Like I said, drivin' us nuts!"

I then asked Bob to quantify—on a scale of one to ten—his level of anxiety (ten being maximum anxiety) during that mortar attack. He thought for a couple of seconds and said it was about an eight. I then asked him to quantify his level of anxiety working for his current boss.

Throwing his head back and raising his arms, he smiled and said, "Great question. It's eleven!"

Amazed, I said, "You're telling me that you're enduring more anxiety now, living in a beautiful home back in the safety of the United States and working for a micromanaging boss than you endured in Afghanistan with random bombs dropping all around you?"

He looked me square in the eye and said, "Yup. That's exactly what I'm saying."

The power of leadership was documented in a fascinating study conducted by the Department of Defense during our wars in Iraq and Afghanistan. Between 2004 and 2010, mental health providers were deployed as part of mental health advisory teams (MHATs) to assess soldier behavioral health, examine the delivery of behavioral health care in Iraq and Afghanistan, and provide recommendations for improvement to high-level decision makers.[3]

In one section of the overall study, twenty-eight platoons on deployment were randomly selected.[4] Researchers assessed the stress level and recorded the cumulative number of combat experiences of each platoon member. Not surprisingly, increases in combat experiences were associated with increases in acute stress scores.

In other words, the more combat a platoon of soldiers was exposed to, the higher their aggregate acute stress score. No surprise there. However, of the twenty-eight platoons studied, there were two that did not follow this pattern. In these two platoons, increases in combat experiences did *not* increase their acute stress scores. In fact, in the case of some soldiers within these two platoons, stress levels actually *decreased*. In other words, soldiers in these two platoons appeared to be more resilient to combat than soldiers of the other twenty-six platoons. This finding intrigued MHAT members. Was this simply an anomaly, or was there something else going on in these two "resilient" platoons?

To gain more insight into these inconsistencies, MHAT members interviewed soldiers from the two resilient platoons. One intriguing discovery emerged from these conversations. Soldiers in both platoons uniformly stated that they loved their respective platoon leaders. They felt as if their leader cared for them. MHAT members mused over a fascinating question: Could strong leadership create a more resilient soldier?

To test this hypothesis, MHAT members identified a cohort of 638 soldiers who had experienced intense and sustained levels of combat.

They wanted to find two pieces of data on each of these soldiers: (1) Did the soldier have symptoms of posttraumatic stress disorder (PTSD) diagnosis? (2) Did the soldier rate their leader with "positive satisfaction" (i.e., their leader cared) or "negative satisfaction" (i.e., their leader was uncaring)? Again, to be clear, this is not to say that these leaders *were* uncaring. However, their actions and behaviors were such that the soldiers *perceived* them as uncaring.

The results were startling.

Of those soldiers who rated their leaders positively, only 7 percent met the criteria for diagnosis of PTSD.

Of those soldiers who rated their leaders negatively, an astounding 45 percent met criteria for a PTSD diagnosis.

The data suggests a *sixfold* difference in incidence of PTSD based on the effectiveness of the leader among this cohort of soldiers. The researchers concluded that "positive officer leadership is the key factor providing soldier well-being and resiliency from high combat."[5]

This data certainly illuminates the power of leadership. The sheer magnitude of these findings is amazing. If the quality of a leader can indeed decrease the likelihood of a person manifesting symptoms of PTSD after a traumatic event, how powerful *is* the leadership phenomenon?

As mentioned in the previous chapter, I've learned that leaders grossly underestimate how their behaviors as leaders, specifically showing that they care, impacts trust. As mentioned, this could be due to the flood of research, data, articles, and books on the topic of leadership that has diluted the importance of building trust. Or it could be because leaders are simply overwhelmed with other prerogatives. Regardless of reason, in order to be inspired to employ the behaviors described in this book— behaviors that convey care and compassion and consequently earn more trust—it is vitally important that leaders understand how the relationships between caring, trust, and performance are inexorably intertwined. The more caring, the more trust, the greater the effort. Why is it important? In order for leaders to prioritize caring and relationship building, they need to understand and appreciate this dynamic.

Let's go back to the study. While the researchers did not measure combat effectiveness per se, one could reason that a military unit with fewer soldiers traumatized by combat would be more effective than one heavily populated by soldiers suffering from combat trauma. In fact, history tells us that leaders who took care of their soldiers led units that were the most combat effective.[6] In other words, the more caring, the more trust, the greater the effort.

Upon transitioning from the Navy, I worked for a time as a leadership development facilitator for a corporation. My learning on the topic of leadership continued, and the job was a good fit. One aspect that I loved was researching well-conducted studies that proved the link between behaviors of the leader, team culture, and team performance. I was thrilled, and I suspect Chief Tandy, cousin Steve, and Chief Smock would have been similarly excited, to find ample proof that what we had collectively experienced over our combined hundred-plus years of naval service was supported by solid research.

In my research I came across a fascinating company that has been studying workplace culture for as long as I have—thirty years. However, they've discussed leadership with a few more people than I have. In fact, they've surveyed over one hundred million employees over that thirty-year span. Their goal is to help organizations build high-trust, high-performing workplace cultures. The company is the Great Place to Work (GPTW) Institute. They are considered the global authority on building, sustaining, and recognizing high-trust, high-performing workplace cultures. Like me, they believe that when leaders take care of their employees, great things happen. With access to reams of data, they set out to prove it.

In the late 1990s, *Fortune* magazine asked the GPTW team to develop an annual list of the best companies to work for in the United States. What resulted was the annual "Fortune 100 Best Companies to Work For" list, which is published each year in the magazine's January edition. To compile the list, the GPTW Institute surveys two million people and gathers data on the culture of nearly six thousand companies worldwide each year. They use a consistent methodology: surveys that assess the level of trust, pride, and camaraderie in the company are administered directly to employees.

When trying to ascertain whether a company should be characterized as a great workplace, their research led them to the conclusion that it wasn't *what* the leaders were doing; it was *how* the leaders were doing it. Interestingly, neither the company's business practices nor the amount of money leaders spent on employees had a significant impact on trust, pride, or camaraderie. What mattered was the *relationships* that the leaders built with the employees. In short, what mattered was whether the leader cared for their employees. As a result, companies with caring and engaged leaders enjoyed higher levels of trust, pride, and camaraderie.

The important question is this: When a leader cares, and trust, pride, and camaraderie improve, does this impact overall company performance? In other words, is there a correlation between a caring leader, happy employees, and healthy bottom lines?

At the beginning of my Navy career, I witnessed how Chief Tandy and Chief Smock, through their caring demeanors, profoundly impacted those whom they led. Cousin Steve provided the same wise counsel to me in his own uniquely colorful way. I attribute the success that we enjoyed at Naval Hospital Bremerton to my immediate goal of earning my team's trust, specifically by showing that I cared for their well-being. Likewise, during my tour as chief of staff at Navy Medicine West, I attribute the greater success that some commanding officers enjoyed to their embracing the same philosophy. However, were these stories sheer coincidences? It turns out they were not.

From 1998 to 2016, the aggregate annualized stock returns over that eighteen-year period for the companies that were selected for the 100 Best Places to Work list—the companies with high levels of trust, pride, and camaraderie—was nearly three times the market average.[7]

How can this be explained? When leaders implement practices that contribute to strong employee-employer relationships, employees feel as if their leaders care and, therefore, they have a great workplace experience. This results in strong employee engagement that, in turn, results in top performance and healthy bottom lines. When employees feel that their leader cares, they enjoy high levels of trust, which results in fewer disruptions, less stress, and greater focus on the job at hand. Employees will be more creative—they will be inspired to speak up to improve processes and procedures. Companies in turn enjoy lower staff turnover, more qualified candidates for positions, and lower absenteeism. In other words, a caring leader is a more trusted leader, and people work hard when they trust their leader.

I've witnessed the impact of caring leaders throughout my career, both while in the Navy and after. This was especially the case during a short period when, after my Navy career, I worked for a university in Southern California. The job required me to meet the managers of hundreds of retail pharmacies throughout the L.A. area. While I visited store managers of hundreds of stores, each was a Costco, Rite Aid, CVS, or Walgreens store. Each CVS store, for example, had nearly the exact same layout, product positioning, and store design as all the other CVS stores. While these stores looked like carbon copies, the level of customer service was anything but consistent; each was quite different.

Prior to meeting the store manager, I'd spend a few minutes wandering the store to observe how the employees treated customers. Some stores had tremendous customer service. Other stores . . . well, it was sometimes painful to watch! Here's what I found fascinating: *Every* store that had employees who engaged the customer with a smile, joy, and confidence had a manager who was, well, joyful, smiling, and confident. Likewise, *every* store where I witnessed aloof, disrespectful, harried employees was led by a manager who—you guessed it—acted in the exact same manner.

The behaviors of the employees and their managers were eerily similar. Was this a coincidence, or was there something more to it? Given that customers can choose where they shop, I also wondered if the stores led by the smiling, engaging managers were more profitable than those led by the frowning, angry managers. I began searching for studies that could answer these questions.

In answer to the first question—why did the behaviors of the employees and their managers mirror one another?—a study by Gallup found that leaders' engagement directly influences their employees' engagement, creating what Gallup calls the "cascade effect."[8] The link between the two is powerful. In fact, employees who are supervised by highly engaged managers are 59 percent more likely to be engaged than those supervised by actively disengaged managers. In other words, the engaging behaviors of the leader were emulated by the employees.

In another study, researchers wanted to know if a leader's level of humility influenced their subordinates' level of humility.[9] They found that a leader's humility indeed spreads to employees via what they coined a "social contagion," which they found improved team performance.

Leadership Lesson

Numerous studies have shown the profound power of leadership:
- There was a sixfold difference in incidences of PTSD based on the effectiveness of the leader among a cohort of 638 soldiers who had experienced intense combat.
- When employees feel as if their leaders care, their workplace experience, employee engagement, and team performance improve.
- Employees supervised by highly engaged managers are 59 percent more likely to be engaged than those supervised by actively disengaged managers.
- Stores led by caring leaders were significantly more profitable than those led by uncaring leaders.

The researchers concluded that "individuals must act virtuously if they want virtue to spread." In other words, followers generally emulate the behaviors of the leader. These two studies show that what I observed in those chain pharmacy stores was certainly not a coincidence. The employees of those stores were emulating the behaviors of their manager. When we take this to the next logical step, the managers' behaviors created the culture in their stores.

Exactly what is team culture, and how is it created? Team culture is a product of the members' collective behaviors. It's defined by how people on the team interact with one another. Culture is *learned* behavior—it is not created from words in a policy and procedure manual. Who, then, are the team members learning from? As shown in these two studies, they emulate the leaders' behaviors. A leader's actions are exponentially more impactful on culture than any words written in a policy and procedure manual. For example, when a leader's toxic behavior goes unchecked in an organization, it reinforces toxic behaviors down the chain of command. Therefore, it is *the leader* who is teaching others how to behave, and it is *the leader* who creates the culture. This is a key point: leaders create the culture of the organizations they lead. There is much truth to the saying "there are no bad teams, only bad leaders." Indeed, the leader *owns* the culture.

So, what about my other question: Given that people can choose where to shop, were the chain pharmacy stores led by the smiling, engaging managers more profitable than those led by the frowning, angry managers? In other words, do happy employees produce healthy bottom lines? It turns out that Gallup conducted a study to answer this exact question.

In 1997, a successful retailer asked Gallup to measure the level of employee engagement and culture in their three hundred stores across the United States. Like the chain pharmacy stores I visited in L.A., each store had a similar layout, product positioning, store design, and so on.

Gallup asked all thirty-seven thousand employees to complete a well-validated survey of twelve questions (each on a scale of one to five) that measured employee engagement. In essence, these employees were asked if their boss cared for them. In fact, one of the questions on the survey asked, "Does my supervisor care for me?" A total of twenty-eight thousand employees responded to the survey. The scores of employees working at the same stores were aggregated. In this way, employee engagement scores were ascertained for each of the three hundred stores. For example, 65 percent of the employees working in the Boston store felt that their leader cared, compared to only 35 percent in the San Diego store.

Scores were compiled so that the seventy-five stores with the highest employee engagement scores were identified as a cohort and the seventy-five stores with the lowest employee engagement scores were identified as a cohort. Profits were then aggregated for the seventy-five high-engagement stores and the seventy-five low-engagement stores.

The seventy-five high-engagement stores (i.e., stores led by caring

Leadership Lesson

The leader is a social contagion; the leader behaviors are emulated.

> ### Leadership Lesson
>
> The leader creates the culture; the leader owns the culture.

leaders) ended the year almost 14 percent *over* their annualized profit goal. What was the factor that caused employee engagement and profits to climb in these stores? The managers went out of their way to build relationships with their employees—they were engaging, approachable, and caring leaders.

What about the seventy-five low-engagement stores, those stores led by disengaged and uncaring leaders? They *missed* their profit goals by a full 30 percent.

Similar to the GPTW study, stores with happy employees had healthy bottom lines. Based on these studies, I'd speculate that the pharmacies I visited that were led by the smiling, engaging managers were more profitable than those led by the frowning, angry managers.

Can we describe leadership as a "phenomenon"?

The leader's behaviors, good and bad, are emulated by others. This is a very powerful concept, and it gets to the essence of why leadership wields such power and influence. The leader is the primary contagion; their behaviors are infectious. Their behaviors exponentially impact the organization by creating a culture that directly reflects the leader's behaviors and dictates the team's performance level.

There is no question that leadership is profoundly powerful and wields enormous and mystifying influence. It clearly carries enough power and influence to fall into the exclusive domain of a "phenomenon." More importantly, leaders need to be aware of this power and to capitalize on it. All leaders want their teams to be high performing. The data is irrefutable that the key attribute of a high-performing team is trust. When employees trust their leader, they perform at a higher level. The key to earning trust is for the leader to care for their employees. This caring is displayed during the hundreds of interactions the leader has with employees each day. The leader can leverage *each and every one* of these interactions to earn an enormous amount of trust. We'll discuss this further in the next chapter.

KEY POINTS

1. People don't leave bad jobs; they leave bad leaders.
2. Numerous studies have shown the profound power of leadership:
   - There was a sixfold difference in incidences of PTSD based on the effectiveness of the leader among a cohort of 638 soldiers who had experienced intense combat.
   - When employees feel as if their leaders care, their workplace experience, employee engagement, and team performance improve.
   - Employees supervised by highly engaged managers are 59 percent more likely to be engaged than those supervised by actively disengaged managers.
   - Stores led by caring leaders were significantly more profitable than those led by uncaring leaders.
3. The leader is a social contagion; the leader behaviors are emulated.
4. The leader creates the culture; the leader owns the culture.

3

INTERACTIONS

Opportunities to Earn Trust

> It means a lot to me when I put my hand in the dirt on third-and-inches, that my coach cares about me as a person, not just as a player . . . it gives me that extra drive when you're tired and it's your off day . . . you don't want to come in but you realize how much he cares about you.
>
> —Barry Cofield, former professional football
> player for the Washington Redskins

I was reading the sports section of *USA Today* on a flight a few years ago when I came across an article about an NFL team, the Washington Redskins.[1]

In the article was the above quote from Barry Cofield, then a star defensive player on the team. Cofield was talking about his head coach, Mike Shanahan, and it was clear from those words that Cofield was very passionate about playing football for his coach.

I was still in the military at the time, and, after reading the quote, I thought with a bit of envy, "I'd like all my people to say that about me."

I noted that Cofield mentions the word "cares" twice. Thinking about Chief Tandy, cousin Steve, and Chief Smock, as well as my readings about the power of the caring leader, I quickly read on. I wanted to know specifically what Coach Shanahan did to garner this level of motivation from Cofield. Based on this quote, it seems that Cofield would walk through a wall for Coach Shanahan. At six feet four inches and three hundred–plus pounds, Cofield probably could! Did Cofield's loyalty emanate from a new defensive scheme that Coach Shanahan cooked up to help Cofield maximize his talent? Was it Cofield's renegotiated multimillion-dollar contract? Or was it something much simpler? What did Coach Shanahan do to get Cofield to give it that "extra drive"?

It was simply this: Coach Shanahan showed interest in his players.

According to the article, during summer camp that year, Cofield informed Coach Shanahan that his grandfather had passed away and that he wanted to go home to attend the funeral. He wanted to be with his family.

Summer camp in professional football is an extremely important part of the season. Members compete fiercely for positions and playing time. The team learns a plethora of plays and bonds as a unit. Missing any part of summer camp is strongly discouraged.

What did Coach Shanahan do in response to Cofield's request?

He told Cofield to go to the funeral and take as much time as he needed with his family. Shanahan then informed the team, with Cofield's permission, of Cofield's absence and the reason for it. Shanahan finished by reminding the team that, to him, family was number one.

Why was Cofield so fired up to play for Coach Shanahan? Why did Cofield believe his coach cared about him so much? When asked, that was the story Cofield told.

Many leaders, myself included, would have looked at the situation Coach Shanahan faced as a dilemma. Maybe he did. Regardless, he did the right thing. By doing so, Coach Shanahan showed his player that he truly cared about him, and Cofield loved him for it. Coach Shanahan had a difficult decision to make during this interaction with one of his key players, the end result being vastly improved trust.

Where are the opportunities for a leader to show that they care?

When I ask this question at my leadership seminars, participants inevitably reply with a host of answers—one-on-one meetings, social events, email, and so on—*all* of which, by the way, are true. The answer is this: there are *hundreds* of opportunities each day to show that you care. *All* interactions between the leader and their subordinates are such opportunities. Consequently, *all* interactions are opportunities to display behaviors that earn trust. Certainly, some interactions will be more impactful than others. But each and every interaction should be considered an opportunity.

Leadership Lesson

All interactions between the leader and their subordinates are opportunities for the leader to display behaviors that earn trust.

Think about the power of this maxim. A leader has hundreds of interactions with members of the team every day on an hour-by-hour, minute-by-minute, second-by-second basis. Opportunities are abundant, and all of them can incrementally earn trust and, consequently, improve workplace culture and team performance.

How does this work? Team members observe the leader's behaviors during interactions and consciously and subconsciously analyze each of them. The leader's behaviors are constantly being scrutinized. Often they are quietly discussed among team members. From this process, one of two conclusions are drawn: either the leader cares and more trust is earned or the leader doesn't care and trust is lost. The building or eroding of trust is volatile. While some interactions will impact this dynamic more than others, *all* will have an impact.

The great leaders understand, respect, and embrace this maxim: their behavior during each and every interaction determines whether they will be perceived as caring and trustworthy. In fact, they leverage this reality and create *more* interactions between themselves and their team members. Great leaders recognize that team culture and, ultimately, team performance will be driven accordingly.

Unfortunately, not all leaders share this understanding. Even seasoned leaders get this wrong, and numerous opportunities to improve trust are lost. Let me give you a couple of examples of leaders who got it right and others who got it wrong.

A couple of years ago, my wife and I were traveling in Europe and visited a close personal friend, Rick, who was employed as a public affairs officer on a U.S. military base. One evening my wife and I attended a spouse abuse awareness event that took place on the military base. Rick was covering the event to take photos and write an article for the base's newspaper. The event, attended by about fifty people, began with a beautiful prayer delivered by the base chaplain. The base commander, an Army colonel with probably twenty-five years of leadership experience, was the next speaker.[2]

The colonel made appropriate remarks. However, in the middle of her remarks, she mentioned that, before the ceremony, she had reviewed the chaplain's prayer and thought some changes needed to be made. She went on to say that she requested that the chaplain make a minor change to the wording of the prayer. I happened to be looking at the chaplain when these remarks were made. His face showed both embarrassment and resentment.

Here was a very quick interaction that provided the colonel with an opportunity to say some kind words and build up the chaplain's confidence, an act of caring that would have improved their relationship. Instead, she added a few words to make herself look smarter at the expense of the chaplain. Instead of improving the relationship, she damaged it. The culture moved toward one of fear because of this brief display of disrespect.

At the conclusion of the event, Rick introduced my wife and me to the colonel and the command sergeant major (CSM).[3] In front of Rick, the CSM, my wife, and me, the colonel stated that Rick had done a good job for her. However, right on the heels of those complimentary words, the colonel mentioned that once, in the past, she had to tell Rick not to publish a certain article in the base's newspaper. As soon as she said this, I noticed the CSM lower his head in anger and embarrassment. Needless to say, this was an awkward moment for all of us. The CSM was acutely aware of not only the opportunity lost but also the damage done. Out of the corner of my eye, I noticed Rick drop his head in embarrassment.

This was an opportunity to say complimentary things about a key staff member in front of his close friends. It was one of those golden opportunities to improve a vitally important relationship. Reminding an employee of a past indiscretion in front of anyone, especially a close friend, is ruinous to a trusting relationship. As you can imagine, Rick reacted with anger. This brief, two-minute interaction resulted in unnecessary humiliation and distrust. While this may seem like an extreme example of poor leadership, I came away wondering how often this type of interaction occurred. The end result was diminished trust between the colonel and her team.

During my command tour, I made a habit of scheduling thirty-minute meetings with each staff member from my command who was returning from an Individual Augmentee deployment in support of the global war on terror.[4] I scheduled these meetings for a number of reasons, not the least of which was to assess them for reintegration issues that are common when a military member returns from deployment. Posttraumatic stress disorder and family reintegration issues were the most common.[5] I also wanted to learn of their experiences during their deployment. I loved hearing their stories, and they loved telling them. Being fascinated with leadership, I often asked about their leaders. I almost always came out of these meetings feeling very excited and motivated. These young men and women performed incredible deeds in the service of our country in about as austere an environment as one could imagine. I knew our country was in fine hands with these remarkable service members, the vast majority of whom were in their early twenties.

Within a few seconds of their entry into my office, and without them having to utter a word, I could tell immediately if their deployment was an overall uplifting or, sadly, a disappointing experience. Their body language revealed the truth. The good news is that the vast majority of these amazing young men and women found these deployments to be positive experiences.

One morning in the late fall of 2008, my secretary, Dawn, greeted me with her usual smile and reviewed my itinerary for the day. Knowing that meeting with sailors returning from deployment was one of my most joyous highlights as a commanding officer, Dawn gleefully informed me that I was to meet with two such sailors that day.

"It's going to be a good day!" I thought at the prospect of spending some time with these young sailors. Prior to meeting with them, I briefly discussed details of their deployments with a few other members of my command. I learned that one of the sailors had recently returned from a challenging deployment to Iraq. I was told that the sailor had been assigned to an Army Mortuary Affairs unit.[6] If true, this was concerning to me. While the service provided by these teams is extremely important—many of our men and women killed in the line of duty are identified and laid to rest with great solemnity and reverence due to these teams' tireless efforts—it also comes with a cost. Studies have shown that Mortuary Affairs personnel have some of the highest rates of posttraumatic stress disorder.[7] Evidence suggests that those involved with the removal and disposal of war dead often have to deal with significant psychological pressure later on in their lives as well as at the time of their duties. Interestingly, years ago, my late father-in-law, Corporal Dan Sexton, United States Army, told me of his brief experience with work in a similar unit during his service in Korea during the Korean War. He never provided details. However, he made it clear that it was very psychologically challenging work. Nevertheless, like millions of U.S. service members before and after Corporal Sexton's service in the Korean War, these men and women unselfishly and stoically do what needs to be done.

The other sailor whom I was to meet that day had just returned from deployment on the hospital ship United States Naval Ship (USNS) *Mercy* in support of Pacific Partnership 2008,[8,9] a humanitarian mission that provided health care to poor and indigenous civilian populations ashore in Vietnam, Cambodia, Indonesia, and Timor-Leste. I had met and spoken to many sailors who had deployed on earlier Pacific Partnership missions. Many of these sailors literally cried tears of joy as they told me heartwarming stories of providing medical care to hundreds of sick children on poor Pacific islands. They were profoundly appreciative of the opportunity to help hundreds of underserved men, women, and children, and many described these experiences as life changing. I was excited that morning to hear of a deployment full of heartwarming stories of meaningful, impactful work.

While I was aware that I would be meeting one sailor who had been deployed on the USNS *Mercy* and another who had been assigned with the Army Mortuary Affairs unit in Iraq, I didn't know which one had been on which deployment.

The first sailor entered my office. His overall body language conveyed confidence and joy. Although he stood ramrod straight, his body appeared relaxed. He looked me in my eyes and smiled casually.

"Good morning, sir. It's a pleasure seeing you again, sir!" he said confidently as we shook hands. I noted that he shook my hand with a firm grip.

"HM3 Fox reporting as requested, sir!"[10] he said with a hint of self-assuredness.

"Great," I thought, "I'm going to hear some wonderful stories of the care this young sailor provided to indigenous South Pacific Islanders."

After a hearty "Welcome home, shipmate" and other pleasantries, I asked HM3 Fox to tell me of his deployment on the *Mercy*.

His head shot back, and with a confused look he said, "*Mercy* . . . I didn't deploy on the *Mercy*, sir. I just returned from Iraq."

Trying to disguise my surprise, I fumbled a bit with a heartfelt apology. My initial surprise quickly changed to curiosity. Did I have the right information regarding his deployment? Had HM3 Fox been assigned to an Army Mortuary Affairs unit? My initial impression of this sailor certainly didn't indicate any signs of distress. I hastily asked him to tell me the story of his deployment.

With appropriate somberness, he told me that he had been deployed to Iraq and had indeed worked in Mortuary Affairs. He told me with the perfect balance of humbleness and pride that his unit's job—to retrieve, identify, and transport deceased American and American-allied military personnel as well as Iraqi soldiers and civilians—was certainly grim but of vital importance.

"This was tough stuff," I thought. However, he had such a positive attitude. It piqued my curiosity.

I then asked, "Tell me about your boss."

"Oh, yeah," he said with growing enthusiasm, "let me tell you about my sergeant! My sergeant was awesome!"

He proceeded to tell me how his sergeant repeatedly told him and other members of the team how vitally important their jobs were. With obvious pride, he recited to me that they were responsible for the proper preparation, preservation, and shipment home of the remains of not only U.S. and allied service members but also Iraqi service members and civilians. HM3 Fox took special pride in describing to me how important it is in the Muslim religion to complete burial ceremonies as soon as possible, preferably within twenty-four hours from the time of death, and how his team did everything possible to honor that practice out of respect for the people of Iraq.[11]

"Sir," he enthusiastically stated on more than one occasion, "my sergeant told me that we had to win the hearts and minds of the Iraqi people. He told us, sir, that winning hearts and minds was very important, and we can't win hearts and minds if we don't respect their religious practices."

He continued with soaring pride, "Sir, we were able to honor this practice *every* time. My sergeant told us that we did a good job and that our work was very important, sir."

Their work was indeed important. During the time of MH3 Fox's deployment, the United States had revised its strategy in Iraq. The new strategy was to implement counterinsurgency operations to win the war in Iraq.[12] Winning the hearts and minds of the Iraqi people was indeed the primary objective to win the war. I was a bit speechless. This impressive young man, probably in his midtwenties, was thrown into a horrific situation and came out, by all accounts, a much more confident, satisfied, and stronger person. He was extremely proud of what he and his team had accomplished as a result of their collective efforts.

It was clear that his sergeant was responsible for the unit's well-earned pride. What did the sergeant do? As our conversation continued, I learned that during numerous formal and probably just as many random and informal interactions, the sergeant simply took some time to explain to HM3 Fox the importance of the job. The sergeant employed a simple but very powerful—and, unfortunately, often forgotten—tenet of leadership. He did what I like to call "connecting the dots." In very simple terms, HM3 Fox's sergeant cared enough to take the time to explain why the job was important. Despite the very grim nature of his work, HM3 Fox found profound fulfillment from the deployment. His sergeant clearly cared enough to take the time to keep his subordinates informed—not only of their importance to the organization but also of his gratitude. Making that extra effort showed that he truly cared about his subordinates, which earned their trust.

Regardless of how seemingly menial a task, all tasks are connected to a greater cause. Outstanding leaders take the time to make that connection for their employees, and they demonstrate their gratitude and respect in the process. They connect the dots. The leader cares that their people understand how their task, however seemingly menial or insignificant, fits into a bigger cause. Whether it's an organizational change, a decision made, or simply an assigned task, when a leader takes the time to explain the why behind the task, it shows that they care.

Later that afternoon, Dawn informed me that the second sailor, who had deployed on the hospital ship supporting the Pacific Partnership humanitarian mission, was ready to meet with me. Before he came into my office, I thought again about how much fun this conversation would be. I was going to hear some wonderful stories about the care this young sailor had provided to indigenous South Pacific Islanders, just as I had heard from numerous other sailors who had returned from similar life-changing humanitarian missions.

As he entered my office, this sailor's body language told a much different story. Head down, shoulders slumped, he made no eye contact with me. He moved slowly past the doorway into my office. Still no eye contact. He looked down and away from me.

He softly mumbled, "Good afternoon, sir. HM3 Lent reporting."

"Wow," I thought, trying not to look alarmed. "I'm not sure what's going on with this sailor, but it's not good." After a more subdued "Welcome home, shipmate" and other quiet pleasantries, I asked HM3 Lent to tell me about his deployment.

After some gentle prodding on my part, HM3 Lent reluctantly proceeded to mutter that while he enjoyed the few medical civic action projects that he had participated in, as well as visiting some exotic ports, it wasn't what he had expected.[13] He told me, with a hint of bitterness, that he was getting out of the Navy.

I asked him if he understood the importance of what they were doing during the deployment. In fact, these missions are vital to strengthening relationships and security ties between the United States and nations along the Pacific Rim.

He gave me a quizzical look.

"I don't know, sir," he murmured. "I'm sure it's all important . . . helping those poor people. I'm just ready to get outta the Navy."

I asked him to tell me about some of his shipmates. Reluctantly, he proceeded to tell me stories of his immediate supervisor. It wasn't pretty. His leader had micromanaged everyone, threatened and humiliated some, and showed favoritism, among other extremely poor leadership behaviors. HM3 Lent told me that he just avoided his boss as much as possible. He described a leader who was intimidating and led with fear.

Tellingly, on two occasions, HM3 Lent specifically stated, "He [his boss] didn't care."

I've been around long enough to know that there are always two sides to every story. While HM3 Lent had an excellent reputation as a hard worker with a great attitude while at Naval Hospital Bremerton, it's certainly possible that his performance genuinely lapsed at some point during the deployment. While we'll never know the truth of what actually happened between HM3 Lent and his boss, two things were clear. First, even if only some of the reported behaviors of Lent's boss were accurate, they showed very poor leadership. Second, this was clearly a dreadful experience for HM3 Lent. Similar to my experience as a detailer, and as I described in the previous chapter, the culture of fear created by his boss resulted in HM3 Lent being angry, dispirited, and bitter. He was done with the Navy. What opportunities did MH3 Lent's boss miss? A big one was this: Despite hundreds of formal and informal interactions between HM3 Lent and his boss, the boss didn't take time to explain the importance of the job. As opposed to the sergeant in the previous story, HM3 Lent's boss didn't make the effort to illustrate that all their tasks, when put together, connect like pieces of a puzzle toward a greater goal. These types of conversations leave lasting impressions.

Years later, I thought about how the two experiences of these sailors provided a stark example of the power of caring. One can understand how HM3 Fox, after working in a grim job in a forbidding, unsafe environment, could look at that experience as a hardship. However, because his boss cared enough to persistently praise the unit's performance and reinforce the positive importance of their task, the sergeant successfully instilled pride in his subordinates. Conversely, HM3 Lent had a completely different experience. In spite of a much more pleasant work environment and a mission that many sailors would envy—providing health care to extremely poor but exceedingly thankful people in exotic lands—HM3 Lent was led by a poor leader whose actions (and inactions) greatly outweighed the overall experience.

Opportunities for leaders to show they care are abundant, and each act of caring incrementally builds trust. Sometimes these opportunities can be quick, seemingly meaningless, interactions. However brief, they can be extremely uplifting and result in transformational change.

That is exactly what I experienced on the deck of a hospital ship in

---

Leadership Lesson

Whether it's an organizational change, a decision made, or simply an assigned task, take the time to explain the why—it's an act of caring that helps earn trust.

---

the heat of the Persian Gulf in the fall of 1990. I, along with over a thousand other shipmates, was assigned to the new, state-of-the-art hospital ship USNS *Comfort*. We were a small cog within a massive allied coalition that would eventually number nearly one million service members, including seven hundred thousand from the United States. We were all there as a result of Saddam Hussein's sudden invasion of Kuwait in August 1990. It was coined Operation Desert Shield, which turned into Operation Desert Storm and would eventually come to be known as simply the Persian Gulf War. It was on that ship during that deployment when a senior officer had a five-minute conversation with me that completely transformed my attitude. His words were a caring act—they uplifted me—and my trust in him grew exponentially.

On August 2, 1990, the day Saddam invaded Kuwait, I was stationed at Naval Hospital Bethesda in Bethesda, Maryland. Within days of the invasion, rumors were spreading like wildfire throughout the hospital that the USNS *Comfort* would be deploying. This ship had never before sailed into harm's way—this mission would be her first. The majority of her crew would be coming from Naval Hospital Bethesda. The word was that many hospital staff members would deploy. Others would stay. It didn't take long for me to decide which group I wanted to fall in with; I *desperately* wanted to go. I had been trained for this and wanted to use my skills to help in what I considered to be a noble cause.

To give some perspective, at the time of his invasion of Kuwait, Saddam's army was estimated to number one million men, which was the fourth-largest army in the world. During the first few days after the invasion, I watched TV news broadcasts late into those warm August nights as one military expert after another ominously described the size and capability of the Iraqi army. There was very grave concern regarding the elite Iraqi Republican Guard army; reports from Kuwait told of the brutal repression imposed on Kuwaiti citizens by these forces.

The far greater concern was Iraq's extensive chemical warfare program. During the Iran-Iraq war that was fought from 1980 to 1988, a war that resulted in the deaths of an estimated five hundred thousand Iraqi and Iranian soldiers, Iraq used chemical weapons against Iranian troops on numerous occasions. As the war continued into the late 1980s, Iraq's chemical warfare program expanded rapidly.[14] In March 1988, the infamous Halabja massacre occurred, when the Iraqi army used sarin gas and mustard gas on their own citizens.[15] Iraq's biological warfare development pursued a similar course, but by the time Iraqis were testing biological warheads (containing anthrax and botulinum toxin) in Iraq's deserts, the Iran-Iraq war had come to an end.[16]

Given all this, Iraq's invasion of Kuwait shook the world. The United Nations quickly called for an immediate withdrawal of all occupying forces in Kuwait, and an international coalition began to form. Ultimately this coalition would comprise thirty-five countries and would be the largest military alliance since World War II.

Saddam continued to speak defiantly; he declared Kuwait a province of Iraq and vowed not to leave. Further, his armies appeared poised to continue the invasion beyond Kuwait, deep into Saudi Arabia. War appeared imminent, and there was little doubt that casualties would mount quickly if hostilities broke out, especially if Saddam unleashed his arsenal of chemical weapons.

Seeing this drama unfold, I very much wanted to help in this noble cause. Brave men and women would be risking their lives, and I wanted to be a part of a team that would provide the best medical care possible. In addition, despite the fact that I'd only been in the Navy for seven years at that point in my career, I sensed that history was being made and that this could well be the greatest adventure of my Navy career. Given all this, I vowed that I'd do what was necessary to deploy.

On August 9, the rumor of *Comfort* deploying was confirmed. On that day she received an official order to activate. The entire staff at Naval Hospital Bethesda was a flurry of nervous excitement; the great ship would sail! New rumors quickly spread of elusive staffing lists that purportedly directed some staff to deploy and others to remain behind. Chaos reigned as people scrambled to get on one list or off another. In the flurry of activity and excitement, I'm sure some didn't even know what it actually meant to be on either list. In the span of forty-eight hours, my status changed from being on the list to deploy to on the list to stay at least a couple times. As the days passed, the most recent staffing lists—the composition of which seemed to change by the hour—consistently had me staying at the hospital. Regardless, I packed my sea bag, updated my will, and hastily reminded Kris of where our important documents were located. I knew in my heart that I was getting on that ship.

During those dizzying days of early August, I made numerous attempts to convince an array of senior officers of the need to send me on the *Comfort*. None were successful, and at least one senior officer—my boss at the hospital—became agitated with my continued attempts to work every angle to deploy, many of which fell well outside the chain of command. In spite of my dogged and sometimes risky efforts, it appeared that I was to be left behind.

The day came when I pulled up to Naval Hospital Bethesda for work to find a caravan of large buses surrounding the hospital, waiting to take hospital staff to embark on the *Comfort*. My status had not changed; I was not going. Knowing this, I was sickened seeing those buses. I simply couldn't stomach staying behind when this great adventure was within my grasp.

Given the continued changes regarding who was going and who wasn't, I vowed to make one more desperate Hail Mary attempt. The buses were leaving soon, so I knew I had to act fast. I hurriedly climbed the eight floors of the Bethesda hospital tower to make my last-ditch appeal to the person I knew was the "Oz behind the curtain" regarding the creation of the mysterious lists. I was visiting the offices where "the lists" were magically crafted.

Opening the door to the large area, I found people running about, some crazily yelling names and ranks to one another across the room, phones ringing incessantly. It was chaos. I entered the maelstrom, cleared my throat, and approached the desk of Commander Deeter, the senior officer in charge.[17]

Speaking louder than normal to be heard over the bedlam and gathering as much confidence as I could muster, I cleared my throat and said, "Sir . . . excuse me. If I could have a moment of your time. Sir, it appears that I am *not* on the list to deploy. Sir, *that* is a mistake. No doubt with everything you have going on you're not aware that I am the *only* officer capable of . . ." I continued with a feeble attempt to convince him that I had unique knowledge of a new drug information software program that was integral to mission accomplishment for the *Comfort*. While my appeal had a modicum of truth, it was a stretch. A *big* stretch. Desperate times called for desperate measures.

Commander Deeter slowly raised his head from a pile of papers he was nervously shuffling back and forth on his desk. I couldn't help but notice large bags under his eyes, and his eyes were red with fatigue. He was clearly exhausted. He cut me off midsentence and slowly said, "LT Brouker . . . you're . . . not . . . deploying!" He finished with a curt "That is all!"

I turned and slowly left his office, my heart sinking with bitter disappointment. I had given it my best shot but had come up short. I hit the elevator's Down button. As I waited what seemed an eternity for the elevator door to open, a young officer approached me. She introduced herself and told me that she worked for Commander Deeter. She said that she had heard our conversation and continued, "We just had another change to the list. It's been so crazy we haven't had a chance to show Commander Deeter this latest change. LT Brouker, you're on the list to deploy. You're going."[18]

I looked at her in disbelief. Slowly it began to sink in. I realized that this was legit. In a matter of seconds, I went from total dejection to utter elation. My persistence had paid off; I was going!

Within a few days, I found myself on the *Comfort*, in the Persian Gulf, and in a war zone. We had transited the Atlantic Ocean, Mediterranean Sea, Suez Canal, Red Sea, and finally the Gulf of Oman before we passed through the infamous Strait of Hormuz and into the Persian Gulf. Morale on the ship remained high throughout the passage. We, like the vast majority of Americans back home (78 percent of Americans favored the deployment of U.S. forces), were supportive of halting Saddam's brutal invasion of his nonthreatening and peaceful neighbor, Kuwait.[19] I, along with my shipmates, ramped up our confidence and excitement as we began preparing for mass casualties.

As September turned to October . . . and then to November . . . morale, being a fickle mistress, sagged throughout the ship. All teams wrestle with morale that waxes and wanes. Ours was a green crew, and our morale was probably more susceptible to the vagaries of shipboard life. Like sand slipping through one's hand, our initial enthusiasm slowly ebbed away.

One reason for our fading fervor for the deployment was our growing boredom with the multitude of seemingly endless drills that we grudgingly participated in. There were fire drills, man overboard drills, and everyone's favorite, general quarters drills, among others. Donning our MOPP gear was something that we particularly despised. MOPP is an acronym for "Mission Oriented Protective Posture" and is protective gear used during a chemical, biological, radiological, or nuclear strike. Given that we sailed within proximity of Saddam's chemical warfare threat, and certainly would be within range of his SCUD missiles if hostilities broke out, learning how to don and work in our MOPP gear was a necessary evil.[20] This clumsy and heavy gear is normally worn over one's uniform. We needed to learn how to put it on quickly—in a matter of minutes—as the warning time for a chemical attack would be minimal. When in the gear it's hard to hear and movement is excruciatingly slow; you become quickly fatigued with even minor physical tasks. While you're always hot in the Persian Gulf, you're *much* hotter when in MOPP gear. If you wear battle glasses,[21] they'll quickly fog up inside your gas mask. You can't wipe the fog off your glasses because, well, you're wearing a gas mask. The number-one rule during our drills was to wear that damn gas mask—or potentially suffer a horrible death from poisonous gas inhalation. Given Saddam's past propensity for using chemical weapons, donning our MOPP gear was a constant reminder of the true nature of that threat. While there was no large-scale Iraqi employment of chemical weapons during the war, multiple sources provide ample evidence that Iraq did sporadically deploy chemical weapons, including sarin and mustard gas, against coalition forces.[22]

While the seemingly limitless drills, with or without MOPP gear, certainly played a role in sapping our enthusiasm, the primary reason for our fading morale was the paucity of information available to us. Despite the U.S. Postal Services' wise decision to waive the need for postage stamps for any letter sent to or from the Persian Gulf area of operations, mail from home took weeks, sometimes months, to arrive. Regarding news of recent events and happenings, we were in an information vortex. When newspapers came, they were pitifully outdated.[23]

Rumors, gossip, and grumbling filled the information void. In Navy lore it's said that a bitching sailor is a happy sailor. That didn't hold true in our case. There was much bitching and not a lot of happy sailors. Initially I took this all with a grain of salt. However, as the days, weeks, and months plodded by, my enthusiasm waned. Like everyone else on that ship, I dearly missed my loved ones back home—my wife, Kris, and our two-year-old daughter, Shayna. From this toxic milieu grew cynicism, doubt, and a mounting distrust about the wisdom of the whole affair, and I missed Kris and Shayna even more.

Under this fog of boredom, confusion, and rising distrust, I found myself alone early one evening on the rail of the ship, absently witnessing yet another spectacular sunset over the Persian Gulf. Out of the corner of my eye I saw Commander Wink Fisher, one of the surgeons assigned to the ship. He approached me, and, after some pleasantries, I quietly shared my newfound misgivings about the deployment. He listened patiently and then said, "Mark, I don't pay much attention to all the gossip and rumor. I try to focus on my job. The way I see it, my job—our job—is to make sure some kid who gets shot up gets home to his family alive." He paused for a few seconds and looked at me. "That's it."

We remained silent for a few minutes, alone in our thoughts, and eventually we said our goodbyes. Watching the horizon in silence as the countless constellations of stars slowly emerged, I thought about the wisdom of his words. The more I mulled them over, the more clarity I found. Like fog lifting from a morning sun, my cynicism, doubt, and distrust slowly dissipated. Throughout the rest of that deployment, through the air campaign and the ground offensive, as Operation Desert Shield transitioned into Operation Desert Storm, my morale never again wavered. I continued to loathe donning that hot and clumsy MOPP gear, grudgingly participated in the endless drills, and remained in an information vortex—letters continued to take weeks and months to be delivered. The business of rumors, gossip, and grumbling continued to flourish. However, I understood the importance of me being on that ship. My job—our job—was to prevent a mother or father from getting a call that no mother or father should get. It was that simple.[24]

Opportunities for leaders to show that they care are abundant. The words of the leader can uplift, build trust, and create a sense of accomplishment and camaraderie. These interactions can be quick and impromptu but also powerful and transformative. While Commander Fisher's words were very few, they were extremely powerful. Our conversation, our interaction, lasted fewer than five minutes. Nevertheless, in that short span, he took the time to help me find clarity. It was a caring act; his words uplifted me. My trust in the wisdom of our mission and my trust in him as a leader grew and gave me much-needed perspective.

The hundreds of interactions you have daily with team members are all opportunities to display behaviors that can uplift others and show that you care. Certainly, some interactions will be more meaningful than others, but *all* interactions are impactful. The great leaders understand, respect, and fully embrace this important principle. They understand the strong correlation between their behavior, their employees' well-being, team culture, and team performance.

What specific behaviors can a leader easily employ to show that they care and improve trust? Let's find out.

KEY POINTS

1. *All* interactions between the leader and their subordinates are opportunities for the leader to display behaviors that earn trust.
2. Whether it's an organizational change, a decision made, or simply an assigned task, take the time to explain the why—it's an act of caring that helps earn trust.

4

KNOW YOUR STAFF

In companies that don't execute, the leaders are usually out of touch . . . and their people don't really know them.

—Larry Bossidy and Ram Charan,
Execution: The Discipline of Getting Things Done

I was nervous and feeling out of my element that Monday morning. I quickly got dressed in my newest khaki uniform. As I had done every morning for the past twenty years, I checked myself in the mirror. However, on that particular morning, I inspected myself with much greater scrutiny.

Shoes shined. Belt buckle shined. Shirt ironed with crisp military creases.[1] Trousers crisply ironed with standard crease. Collar devices perfectly placed.

"I'm good," I thought, trying to give myself a bit of confidence. I opened the door of my bachelor officer quarters room and headed out.

I was about to spend the next two weeks with fifty of the most impressive professionals I had ever rubbed elbows with up to that point in my life. They were men and women who were at the very top of their leadership game, proven naval leaders who were hand-selected to lead naval commands from around the globe, including the world's most lethal and sophisticated weapons systems—fighter squadrons, aircraft carriers, submarines, and various warships. Their biographies, which I had perused the night before, were extremely impressive. Graduate degrees from Ivy League schools and other top universities were abundant. It was indeed a remarkable group and, at least for the next couple of weeks, I was one of its members.

A few months prior, I had been selected to be executive officer, or XO, of U.S. Naval Hospital Rota, Spain.[2] All fifty of us were similarly selected for major command as commanding officers, executive officers of command, or master chiefs of Navy units around the world.[3] We were all in Newport, Rhode Island, to attend the Navy's prestigious leadership development course known as Command Leadership School.

While I was very excited to attend the class and embark on the most exciting professional journey of my life, I was also a little starstruck. My prevailing thoughts were "Wow, what an amazing group! How the heck did I get here?" Looking back, I guess I was a bit intimidated and probably questioned whether I was worthy to be among this group of leaders.

I arrived for the first day of class that Monday morning at 0750 (7:50 a.m.)—plenty of time to grab a safe seat in the back of the room for the 0800 start, or so I thought.

All these super overachievers had arrived well before me. I'm convinced a few of them did push-ups and sit-ups earlier right there in the room to get the blood going. More concerning, they had taken the choice seats: those in the back of the class. I was stuck sitting in the very first row, which is *not* in my comfort zone. I really don't like being toward the front, and I especially dislike the front row. But there I sat—front and center in the first row.

The first speaker arrived at exactly 0800 and immediately asked the class, "As a leader, when you meet a member of your team for the first time, what do you talk about?"

I sat there, a mere few feet from the speaker, waiting for someone to chime in to answer what appeared to be a pretty simple question.

Silence. Crickets.

I started thinking about what I had done over the past twenty years when I had met new sailors. Given that I'd been relatively successful as a leader during those years, I started feeling a surge of confidence come over me. It was probably a caffeine rush from my third cup of coffee, but it felt like confidence.

"Go ahead, Mark, enlighten them. Maybe even *impress* them. Yeah. I've got this!" were my caffeine-enhanced thoughts.

I bravely raised my hand.

"Yeah, go ahead. What do ya got?" the speaker said, pointing to me.

I cleared my throat and stated with as much poise as I could muster, "You talk about mission, you talk about your vision, you talk about guiding principles."

My bubble of confidence surged as I noted the speaker nodding his head up and down and that my voice, mercifully, didn't crack.

I continued with swelling confidence, "You talk about the hot-button issues, the things that are important to mission accomplishment."

The speaker let me ramble on for another minute or so, head slowly but continuously nodding in apparent agreement.

As I finished, I thought, "Wow, that was easy . . . I think I nailed it. I can hang with this crowd!"

Then the speaker turned to me and said curtly, "That's absolutely wrong. That's not what you talk about."

My bubble burst.

I instantly turned a deep shade of red that was impossible to stop. The more I tried, the more pronounced the redness became. And, oh yes, the blushing was combined with some sweat that appeared on my brow. My fears were realized. I couldn't hang with this crowd.

I regained my composure after a few seconds. My thought then changed to "What was so wrong with my answer?"

What the speaker said next transformed my behavior as a leader and has stayed with me ever since. He explained that what I had said was exactly what most people expected to hear during that first meeting with the boss. They expect to hear of the mission, vision, guiding principles, and so on.

"Every fiber in your body will want to go there," he said, "but resist the temptation. Instead, have them tell you their story." He spelled out in detail how this is best accomplished. Here are four key points:

1. Set the tone for the meeting. Relax and have fun. Explain at the beginning of the meeting that you're going to get to know one another. Next, take a few minutes to tell your story—how did you get to where you are today? Members of your team are interested in your story. Be transparent. Be vulnerable. Be authentic. Also be mindful to not take too much time telling your story. If you have a thirty-minute meeting, take no more

than five minutes to tell your story. This is about them telling their story. It's about them, not you.

2. Ask questions like these: What do you love to do? How did you get to where you are today? What are your short-term (one- to two-year) goals? Where do you see yourself in ten years? What are your dreams and aspirations? What are your expectations of me? Ask about places lived, past jobs, hobbies, challenges. Be sure to ask if you can take some notes—this will help you recall a few important items.

3. Listen well. Listen *very* well. Take a genuine interest and absorb what you're hearing. Don't get distracted. Be disciplined. Assume you have nothing else to do—you simply need to listen. If you find your mind wandering, course correct and refocus. Put your cell phone away, move away from your desktop computer, and remove any barriers (i.e., your desk) between the two of you.

4. Do this exercise with each of your direct reports and other important staff or stakeholders.

After I heard that last piece of advice, I realized how much more effective I would have been in my previous leadership positions if I had heard this earlier in my career. In those previous positions, I had key stakeholders—namely, the comptroller and chief nurse—who were integral to my success.[4] If I had proactively had a "tell me your story" meeting with them, our relationship would have been strengthened much earlier and working with them would have been much easier.

This all piqued my interest. I reflected on the past leaders that I absolutely loved working for—the ones that I worked especially hard for. The ones that I trusted. What did all these great leaders have in common?

They all took a keen interest in me as a person, and their interest was sincere. They knew about me in *all* my roles, including outside of work—as a husband, father, member of the command softball team. What impressed me about these great leaders was that they cared enough to take the time to get to know me. What this all conveyed to me was that they *genuinely* cared for me, not just as a naval officer but also as a person. I grew to trust them earnestly, and I worked *very* hard for them. The more they cared, the more I trusted and the harder I worked.

When these great leaders asked me a question, whether it was about work or just what I had done the previous weekend, they *really* listened to the answer. I've heard the terms "active listening" and "listening with your heart." These great leaders listened with their hearts, and they absorbed what I had to say. Their active listening showed that they genuinely cared.

While I've never had the pleasure of meeting General Colin Powell, I've heard from others who have that one of his many leadership gifts is his tremendous ability to listen. He listens with his heart. People who have spoken with him at social gatherings consistently mention how he made them feel as if they were the only person in the room. This is exactly the reaction a leader is aiming for during these interactions. Make them feel as if they have your full attention throughout the conversation. Care enough to listen with your heart, and you'll lay a solid foundation for a relationship built on trust.

Here's an important warning: The behavior of "getting to know you" is extremely powerful. When the leader listens with their heart, it shows a sincere desire to know about that person—their goals, aspirations, concerns—and conveys an intense level of caring. However, if you're easily distracted, reading text messages on your phone or emails on your computer, you'll come off as insincere. The result will be a detriment to trust and, depending on how disingenuous your behaviors are, possibly a significant detriment. If you know you'll have a difficult time staying focused during a meeting—whether due to a pressing business issue or a family concern—reschedule it. Be transparent and explain why you have to reschedule.

Thinking about this during my two weeks of training in Newport, I began to appreciate the potential power of proactively knowing your staff. Had I made an effort to know my staff up to that point in my career? No. Not really. While there were some staff members that I had come to know a bit, mostly through quick conversations during rare breaks in busy pharmacy operations, I certainly didn't *proactively* spend time getting to know them.

The simplicity of this strategy also resonated with me. It required only time and discipline. Time to get to know them. Discipline to sched-

---

Leadership Lesson: Tell Me Your Story

- Set the tone for the meeting by first telling your story. Take no more than a couple of minutes. Be disciplined; this is about them, not you.
- Ask them what they love to do.
- Ask, "What are your expectations of me?"
- Ask about short-term goals (one to two years), long-term goals (where they see themselves in ten years), places they've lived, hobbies, concerns, and challenges.
- Listen with your heart. Take a genuine interest and absorb what you're hearing. Don't get distracted. Put your cell phone away, move away from your desktop computer, and remove any barriers (i.e., your desk) between the two of you. Assume you have nothing else to do. If you find your mind wandering, course correct and refocus.
- In addition to direct reports, consider having a "tell me your story" meeting with other key staff and stakeholders.

---

ule the meeting; to avoid slipping into mission, vision, and guiding principles discussions; and, most importantly, to *really* listen to their story. This is clearly not the time to multitask. (This last point about avoiding the temptation to multitask may appear obvious, but the danger is so severe that it warrants mentioning.)

I was eager to implement this behavior as soon as I could at Naval Hospital Rota.

Upon reporting to the hospital, I was happy to learn that my secretary had already scheduled thirty-minute appointments with all newly arrived employees. Two to three one-on-one meetings with new employees were on the schedule each week for my first few weeks. All was set.

To give you a better sense of these meetings, let me give you a little background on the stereotype of a Navy XO. Generally, they are the hardest worker at the command. They are the first to get to work in the morning and the last to leave. They are typically hard-driving, short on pleasantries, and consumers of vast quantities of coffee. If one word were to best describe the XOs that I had worked for up to that point in my career, it would be "intimidating."

Early in my twenty-year Navy career, I had met most of my XOs in similar one-on-one meetings. They'd last fifteen minutes or so. These conversations usually revolved around the CO's mission and vision and how I could support them. Sometimes they would discuss certain areas of focus within my area of responsibility. These meetings were short and businesslike.

Generally, I had two objectives when it came to these meetings with the XO.

First, say nothing to pique their interest. I might need help from the front office after I got myself established (and many times I did), but I certainly didn't want to get on their radar screen from day one. I didn't want to be micromanaged.

Second, gain no additional responsibilities. Like most organizations, Navy commands are always looking for staff members to take on unglamorous duties outside their primary job—for example, being a member of the holiday party committee. The Navy calls these "collateral duties." Eventually I'd certainly "volunteer" for my fair share of these extra duties; however, I first wanted to focus on learning the ins and outs of my primary job.

In my role as XO at Naval Hospital Rota, I well remember the first sailor I met. He was a young enlisted kid, probably early twenties. A few minutes before our scheduled meeting, I peeked around the corner into my secretary's office, where the young man was dutifully sitting. I could see his feet from around my doorway. One leg was nervously bouncing up and down. He was fidgeting with a pen and notebook he had brought to the meeting.

Similar to my experiences meeting XOs in my earlier years, this sailor was probably not looking forward to this encounter. He was very likely dreading the whole affair. It was even more likely that he had the same two objectives I had when I was in his shoes.

I approached the sailor with my hand outstretched and a big smile and bellowed, "Welcome aboard, shipmate. I'm Captain Brouker, and

I'm your XO! Come on into my office. We're going to spend the next thirty minutes getting to know one another."

I invited the sailor to sit down at my round table. I sat in the chair next to him. We faced one another with nothing between us.

"Again, welcome aboard Naval Hospital Rota. Like I mentioned, we're going to spend this time getting to know one another. I'll take a few minutes and tell you about my story, but we'll spend the majority of time having you tell me yours."

Given the stereotype of an XO that I described earlier, one can imagine the look of bewilderment on his face. Eyebrows raised, head pulled back a bit, he was clearly perplexed.

I imagined he was asking himself, "Is this guy for real? Maybe too much caffeine?"

I started by saying, "Let me quickly tell you my story."

I took the next few minutes to tell him how I grew up in the small blue-collar town of Pittsfield, Massachusetts. My father, grandfather, and great-grandfather had all worked in the local General Electric factory. Money was tight, and after high school I lived at home and attended Berkshire Community College while working part-time at a local pharmacy. I was given a huge break when I was accepted to Northeastern University College of Pharmacy in Boston. Being a huge Red Sox and Patriots fan, going to college in Boston was a dream come true. After graduating in 1980, I accepted a job as a retail pharmacist in Washington, D.C. After three years on that job—and two armed robberies—I decided to join the Navy in 1983. (I wagered that Navy pharmacy couldn't be as dangerous as retail pharmacy was in Washington, D.C., in the early 1980s.) I married my wife, Kris, in 1983, and we have three children. I'm a very blessed man.

Finishing, I asked him to tell me his story.

"Yes, sir. Thanks, sir. Well . . . ah . . . I'm from West Virginia, sir. I . . . ah . . . well, I've been in the Navy . . . well, let's see . . . it's been two years now, sir. I joined after graduating from high school. I guess I joined the Navy to see the world, sir," he nervously murmured.

Not much to work with, but it was a start.

"Great—thanks! You're from West Virginia . . . where in West Virginia?"

The conversation struggled along. I asked him about friends and relatives in West Virginia. Who was proud of him back in his home town? Why the Navy and not the Army or Air Force? Hobbies? Favorite sport? Were there any issues with the move to Spain? What were his short-term and long-term goals? I listened intently and paraphrased often, asking questions along the way. While his nervousness abated somewhat as the conversation progressed, he remained guarded.

Our meeting closed, and he left my office looking only slightly less befuddled than he had thirty minutes prior. I've reflected on what that sailor was thinking when he left. It would have been fun to hear some of the conversations he probably had with his shipmates hours and days later.

When asked about his meeting with the XO, I imagine he mused, "It was different, that's for sure. We actually talked about me a lot. He seemed to be interested in me. He asked how the move to Spain went, my past duty stations, where I grew up, my goals and aspirations. We didn't talk about work at all. I don't know . . . it seemed like he cared. We'll see."

Trust certainly wasn't fully established, but the foundation was laid.

A few weeks later I had an interesting encounter with another staff member, a young doctor, who had just reported to the hospital. Lieutenant (LT) Jones had arrived in Spain two days prior to our meeting. As he entered my office for our introductory meeting, I saw the telltale signs of jet lag and the effects of a stressful overseas move. Although LT Jones was in his early thirties, he had bags under his eyes and looked wrung out. While these Navy moves are exciting for the entire family, they also come with a fair amount of stress—lost luggage, misplaced items, children missing friends—among a host of other challenges.

Despite his fatigue, LT Jones perked up as our meeting progressed. We enjoyed a robust conversation, and I learned a great deal about this officer and his young family. However, at the end of the conversation I sensed something was bothering him.

As we were about to close our meeting, I instinctively asked him, "Is there anything I can help you with?"

I noticed his leg start to nervously pump up and down.

He quickly responded, "No, sir. No, sir. I'm good."

"Are you sure?" I asked slowly.

"I guess there is something kinda bothering me, sir . . . but you don't have time to deal with it. It's really nothing, sir. Kinda silly, actually."

Now I was curious. "What is it?" I asked.

"Okay, sir. Well, here's the deal. As I said, my family and I arrived two days ago. We came through Madrid."

He continued, talking faster now, "Everything has gone pretty well with the move so far. Except one thing: You see, sir, we have a dog, and our dog is still somewhere in the airport in Madrid. Apparently she didn't clear customs, and we don't know what to do. We didn't want to miss our connecting flight and simply assumed she would be on our flight to Rota.[5] The truth is, sir, we're not exactly sure *where* our dog is."

Getting more energetic and talking faster, he continued, "Sir, we don't speak Spanish. We don't want to bother anybody. We really want to take care of this ourselves, but we don't even know where to start! For the last two nights, I've come home to an increasingly unhappy family. They keep asking me when we'll get her back!"

Looking visibly relieved and more relaxed, he finished, "That's it, sir. I know how busy you are, and I feel a little weird even telling you this, but you asked, and . . . well . . . that's it, sir."

Reflecting on his plight, it was clear that the longer the situation festered, the more the family would look at this tour of duty as a horrible experience. It would taint their feelings about the Navy in general. Rightly so. Accepting a tour of duty in a foreign country should be a fun and exciting family adventure. Losing the family pet in the move was quickly turning this adventure into a nightmare.

Another cold reality crossed my mind. Across from me was a highly trained doctor with years of education and training. He was jet-lagged and tired from the stress of the overseas move. The missing dog was additional stress he now had to deal with. If this had not yet affected his performance, if left unresolved, it certainly could. It was a big distraction. People struggle to perform at a high level when distracted.

I thanked LT Jones for letting me know of the situation. I confided in him that our family had a dog and two cats, and I would be similarly upset if I were in his shoes.

What does any smart commissioned military officer do when dealing with a challenging situation? Solicit help from the non-commissioned officer (NCO) community! I specifically sought help from the senior NCO assigned to the hospital—the command master chief.

Master Chief Crawford was one of the best leaders I had worked with in my Navy career. In Rota, she seemed to know everybody on the base and treated every sailor in our command as though they were part of her family. More importantly, I recalled her mentioning that she had contacts at the U.S. Embassy in Madrid.

LT Jones and I went to her office, and I quickly briefed her on the situation.

She listened and calmly replied, "I got it, sir."

Master Chief Crawford called me that evening and informed me that the dog was on the next flight to Rota and would be reunited with the family later that evening. She gave me no details, and I didn't ask for any—I've learned that sometimes it's better not to ask.

About three weeks after our conversation, I saw LT Jones, along with his wife and two boys, in the base commissary.[6] He smiled and waved to me. He then immediately bent down and spoke directly to his boys.

I heard him say, "Remember I told you the story of Captain Brouker getting our dog out of Madrid? Well, that's him . . . that's Captain Brouker!"

Before I could say a word about how, in fact, Master Chief Crawford was the true hero in this story, huge smiles came over the kids' faces and they immediately ran over to me and each hugged a leg. I looked at LT Jones and his wife. Both wore similar joyous smiles.

At that moment I realized that I could ask this officer to take on any mission—*any mission*—and he'd probably accept enthusiastically. Equally important, Mrs. Jones would be 100 percent supportive. The level of trust that had formed between us was palpable.

While I relished the moment, the truth, of course, was that Master Chief Crawford worked magic with the chief's mess and got the dog on a flight to Rota in a matter of hours.[7] My simple role was to tell her about it, get out of the way, and not ask questions. (Anecdotally, while I've always been mesmerized by the power of the chief's mess to get things done, to this day this feat stands among the more impressive that I've witnessed in my career. Even now, I have no idea how they pulled it off.)

A few years ago, I gave a leadership seminar in Singapore to a group of young, newly selected corporate leaders. The seminar included a module on this behavior—proactively getting to know your staff. During the question-and-answer session, a young man raised his hand and asked, "So, what you're saying is that we need to . . . well, there's no other way of saying it . . . sort of *get involved* with our employees to help them with some of their personal issues. Is that right?"

I distinctly remember thinking at the time how glad I was that he asked the question. I'm sure others were thinking the same thing. I thanked him and explained that the leader should not take on the responsibility of resolving their employees' personal and professional issues. However, the leader needs to be aware of the issue and inform the employee of resources available that may help resolve it. The leader's role is to *facilitate* resolution, not to take *ownership* of the issue.

This is a very important point. During the course of these conversations with your subordinates, you may hear of some challenges that an employee is facing, similar to what happened during my conversation with LT Jones. As in that example, family issues are common. Again, while you need to be aware of the issue, and give the employee resources to resolve it, you should not take ownership of the issue.

While this story is certainly unique, the fact is that many of our employees wrestle with personal or professional challenges on a daily basis. Grappling with these issues is a distraction—sometimes a major distraction—and distracted employees find it a struggle to perform at a high level. More importantly, recall that every interaction between the leader and subordinate is an opportunity to show that you care—an opportunity to improve trust. If as a leader you take time to help alleviate stress due to a personal or professional challenge, it shows that you care, and confidence in you as a leader will grow among your employees.

About a year after the lost dog incident, I had another fascinating conversation with a dental officer, Lieutenant Commander (LCDR) Williams,

---

Leadership Lesson

The leader's role is to facilitate resolution of a personal issue that an employee has—it is not to take ownership of it.

that further helped me appreciate the profound power of the "get to know your staff" behavior.

As is standard protocol at most naval commands, I met with all officers who had decided to resign their commission (i.e., get out of the Navy before they reached twenty years of active duty service).[8] LCDR Williams had no more obligated service, and he was choosing to get out of the Navy after ten years of active duty service.

I still remember his look of total surprise when I asked him about his short-term and long-term goals. His head shot back, his mouth dropped open, his eyebrows rose. There was an awkward pause.

After a few seconds of silence, he quietly and slowly said, "Sir, this is the first time in my ten years in the Navy that anyone has *ever* asked me about my goals."

He looked at me, and our eyes locked. What he said next was powerful: "Sir, if someone had asked me about my goals in the past, I might be second-guessing my decision to get out."

We'll never know if such a conversation would indeed have changed his career plans. What *was* clear is that my inquiry regarding his goals had a profound impact on him. Since that episode, I more consistently wove inquiries about goals into these conversations. Similar to my experience with LCDR Williams, asking about goals and aspirations takes these conversations to a deeper level. Why? For most people, their life goals are their topmost priority. Asking about them is an extremely effective way to *really* get to know them. It shows that you're making a sincere and conscious effort to understand them, to go beyond the superficial. People have different goals, aspirations, and dreams. By asking about their dreams—and, more importantly, listening to their answers—you're highlighting their uniqueness. You're getting to know them as a person outside of the work environment.

During these conversations I'd also often encourage them to write down both short-term and long-term goals. Studies have shown that people who write down their goals are more likely to reach them compared to those who do not.[9] Researchers have also found that goal setting is one of the simplest, most straightforward, and highly effective techniques for motivating employee performance.[10] In one study, researchers found that an easily administered goal-setting intervention produced improvements in academic success among struggling university students.[11] In another large study that included forty thousand participants in eight countries, researchers found that articulating specific difficult goals increased performance on over one hundred different tasks.[12]

During my last tour of duty as chief of staff, Navy Medicine West, I spent about thirty minutes with each newly assigned commanding officer in our headquarters in San Diego with one goal in mind: I wanted us to get to know one another. Of course, I also encouraged them, in turn, to employ this behavior with their senior leaders at their respective commands. I also shared the important tips every leader needs to remember: be genuine, listen with your heart, and be mindful that no one is going to tell you to stop talking, especially in your powerful role as commanding officer. I warned each CO that some staff members will let them—and subtly encourage them—to monopolize the conversation for the entire thirty minutes. While they'll appear engrossed in the detailed account of the CO's latest 5k race, they're not. They're asking these questions because they don't want to open up. They're "running out the clock"—letting you chew up the entire thirty minutes. Maybe they're shy. Maybe they're nervous. Maybe they don't trust you. Maybe a little of all three—or something else. Either way, I implored each CO to remember this important truth: it's a rare employee who will tell the boss to stop talking. (We'll discuss this topic in much more detail in chapter 6.)

Unfortunately, one of our commanding officers missed the point about talking too much. He spent the majority of the thirty minutes talking about himself—career highlights, goals, and so on. What's worse, when the staff member finally had their five minutes to tell their story, the CO would periodically glance at their computer screen. Not surpris-

Leadership Lesson

Asking an employee about their goals is an extremely effective way of showing that you care, that you want to go beyond the superficial to *really* get to know them. You will also motivate them and improve their chances of achieving their goals.

ingly, this command required more attention from our headquarters than others.

Why does having this kind of initial one-on-one conversation show that you care?

First, you're spending time getting to know them as a person. You're placing a priority on building a relationship with them. Your employees know you're busy, but, in spite of numerous other tasks, urgent and otherwise, you're spending your time getting to know them. When you listen with your heart—paraphrasing, asking questions, or perhaps providing guidance regarding reaching their goals and aspirations—the message is clear: you care.

Second, you're being transparent. By telling *your* story, you're being vulnerable. Interestingly, when I ask participants at my leadership seminars to list behaviors of leaders whom they loved working for, being transparent and vulnerable is almost always mentioned. Take this time as an opportunity to be both.

In my experience and research, the method of proactively taking time to get to know your staff is *the* most powerful behavior a leader can employ to help build a foundation of trust—it greatly expedites the process.

What skills does a leader need to employ it? Time and the ability to listen.

While we discussed the importance of listening skills earlier in this chapter, you might still be asking yourself one pressing question in particular: Is the thirty minutes or so that is required to get to know your employee a good investment of time? Recall the data from chapter 2 regarding the strong correlation between a leader's level of engagement and team performance. Companies led by leaders who built trust by caring for their employees had aggregate annualized stock returns that were nearly three times the market average over an eighteen-year period. In another study that assessed employee engagement in three hundred identical retail stores, researchers found that the seventy-five stores with the highest scores (i.e., stores led by caring leaders) ended the year almost 14 percent *over* their annualized profit goal, while the seventy-five stores with the lowest employee engagement scores (i.e., those stores led by disengaged and uncaring leaders) missed their profit goals by a full 30 percent. A relatively small investment in time—a one-on-one meeting

> ## Leadership Lesson
>
> Taking time to proactively get to know your staff is *the* most powerful behavior a leader can employ to expedite the trust-building process.

dedicated to getting to know the employee—is an act of caring that reaps an impressive return. A caring leader is a more trusted leader, and people work hard when they have more confidence in their leader.

Very early in my command tour, I was able to use this behavior to completely transform a vitally important relationship with one of my key staff members. Our relationship went from adversarial to trusting. What caused this dramatic change? We took time to get to know one another and, as a result, ended up building a relationship that ultimately helped us accomplish our mission.

During my first week in command, the director of Nursing Services came into my office with a look that can only be described as shock and horror. She informed me that some of our civilian contracted intensive care unit (ICU) nurses (civilians employed under contract) were threatening to go on strike. I remember trying desperately to maintain my composure as my stomach churned. Here was my first crucible moment in command.

Naval Hospital Bremerton had a very strong union presence. I was informed of this well before assuming command. Given that, being confronted with a labor dispute at some point in my tour was to be expected. However, I didn't expect it during my first week, so it came as a bit of a surprise. Perhaps the union was testing the new CO.

The issue was that the ICU nurses believed they were underpaid. After researching salaries for ICU nurses in the Bremerton area, we discovered that our ICU nurses were indeed paid slightly less. After deliberating with my board of directors, I decided to give them a raise, and the strike was averted. More importantly, the next day I had my secretary make an appointment to have the union head, Charles, meet with me in my office.

The following week Charles came to my office for our meeting. I recall him shaking my hand with an extra firm grip, his right arm moving back and forth in an exaggerated manner—I suspected he was sizing me up. To be honest, I guess I was doing the same to him. We awkwardly exchanged pleasantries, but the air was filled with suspicion, tension, and mistrust. It was palpable. I thanked him for coming and then stated in simple terms the reason for the meeting—I simply wanted to get to know him. His head shot back, and he looked at me, perplexed. After a few clumsy seconds, he said, "Okay, sounds good," but his words and body language conveyed cynicism. Over the next hour, our discussion touched on a wide variety of topics—where we grew up, high school years, and hobbies, among a host of others. One topic that monopolized the conversation was our families. We shared a deep love and commitment to our families. Notably, neither of us made reference to the elephant in the room—the averted strike.

Initially, though, our words were guarded and we remained in a defensive mode—we were still sizing each other up. However, as we continued to exchange stories and the minutes ticked by, without either of us realizing it, our relationship began to change. Like snow melting in the warming spring sun, our defensive posture began to thaw—we became a bit less uncomfortable with one another. We were still guarded, but our relationship had undergone a change. With a couple minutes left in our meeting, and still no mention of the averted strike, I suggested to Charles that we meet again. He quickly agreed. As he left my office, our eyes locked. It was time to address the elephant in the room.

I looked at Charles and said, "I gave the nurses a raise because their pay was less than others in the area. It was a reasonable request. I'll *always* consider reasonable requests."

Charles slowly nodded in agreement. As we shook hands, I continued, "Charles, our country's at war. You know as well as I do, we have a lot of folks from here who are deployed.[13] We have an important mission to accomplish here. I need your help." He nodded in agreement, said nothing, and left my office. While I can't speak to how Charles viewed that first meeting, I felt assured that we could begin to build a relationship to mutually benefit the people we represented and, more importantly, the command.

After that initial meeting, Charles and I got together each month.

Like something out of a *Godfather* movie, we'd spend the first fifty-five minutes talking about our families. Only at the end of the meeting, with a couple minutes left, we'd talk business. Over the ensuing months, with every meeting, our mutual respect, friendship, and trust grew.

In fact, at the end of one meeting, Charles "suggested" that I look into something. He went on to explain that the housekeeping staff had been waiting over six months for a new type of linen cart. Apparently, while the new cart wasn't that much more expensive than the carts currently in use, the new cart was configured to significantly reduce back strain for the housekeeping staff. After Charles left my office, I immediately approached my XO, Commander Kurt Houser. I told him of the situation and let him know of my plan—if the information proved accurate, I'd like to get the cart onboard and in use prior to my next meeting with Charles. Both Kurt and I knew that this was a great opportunity to further strengthen my relationship with Charles.

Kurt quickly verified that the purported benefit of the new carts was indeed accurate. He found the purchase order for the new carts and expedited their purchase and delivery. The carts were onboard within a couple of weeks—*before* my next scheduled meeting with Charles.

During our next meeting, Charles and I conducted our business according to our established routine. As the meeting was coming to a close, Charles got up to leave my office, turned to me with a smile, and thanked me for getting the new linen carts onboard. I looked at him and said, "Thank you for bringing it up to me. Purchasing them was the right thing to do for our staff. Remember our first conversation. The linen cart was a reasonable request. I'll *always* consider reasonable requests."

Despite a rocky start when the ICU nurses threatened to strike during my first week in command, Naval Hospital Bremerton did not have another labor dispute during my ensuing three years in command. Not only did we avoid any additional labor disputes, but Charles and I worked closely on a number of difficult and challenging issues. Our respect and trust continued to grow. All issues were resolved quietly and quickly. I helped him, and he helped me.

The overall experience proved to me once again that the small investment of time—and the all-important ability to listen—required in getting to know your people produces inordinate returns. Proactively taking time getting to know your people is an extremely powerful leadership behavior.

Despite its profound power and ease of use, I find that this behavior is woefully underutilized. My experience, as well as solid research, shows that organizations that inculcate this behavior into their culture set themselves apart from others. It is a major competitive advantage for any organization.

Proactively getting to know your staff is an extremely powerful behavior. There is no faster way to help build a solid foundation of trust. However, as mentioned earlier, additional behaviors must be employed to build on that foundation.

KEY POINTS

1. When meeting to have the employee tell you their story:
   - Set the tone for the meeting by first telling your story. Take no more than a couple of minutes. Be disciplined—this is about them, not you.
   - Ask about short-term goals (one to two years), long-term goals (where they see themselves in ten years), places they've lived, hobbies, concerns, challenges.
   - Ask them what they love to do and what *their* expectations are of *you*.
   - Listen with your heart. Take a genuine interest and absorb what you're hearing. Don't get distracted. Put your cell phone away, move away from your desktop computer, and remove any barriers (i.e., desk) between the two of you. Ask permission to take notes. This will help you recall a few important facts.
   - In addition to direct reports, consider having a "tell me your story" meeting with other key staff and stakeholders.
2. The leader's role is to facilitate resolution of a personal issue that an employee has—it is not to take ownership of it.
3. Asking an employee about their goals is an extremely effective way of showing that you care, that you want to go beyond the

superficial to really get to know them. You will also motivate them and improve their chances of achieving their goals.

4. Taking time to proactively get to know your staff is *the* most powerful behavior a leader can employ to expedite the trust-building process.

5

BE VISIBLE

Distance is a negative dimension. The man who insists on it
becomes a recluse, and the reclusive commander achieves
nothing.

—John Keegan, *The Mask of Command*

At one point during my command tour there emerged a growing
threat that the federal government was going to shut down due to
an ongoing congressional budget crisis.[1] The leadership team at the hospital worked hard to create contingency plans to minimize the impact
on our patients. However, if the government did shut down, we were
all aware that almost one-third of the hospital workforce—about four
hundred government service civilian employees—would be furloughed.
They'd be out of work with no pay. As you can imagine, everyone,
especially the four hundred civilian employees, were extremely concerned.

I kept all staff—and certainly the four hundred civilian employees—
updated on any information I received from our headquarters. All emails
on the topic were immediately forwarded to them. Everyone had all the
information I had. However, there were many unanswered questions,
primarily because there had not been a similar budget crisis—with the
threat of a government shutdown—in a number of years. Many of us
were in uncharted waters, and the folks with the answers and who
decided policy were well up the chain of command.

As the drumbeat for a possible shutdown continued, my executive
officer, Captain Ken Iverson, advised me to schedule a series of lunchtime meetings between myself and the civilian employees. He thought it

important that they have the opportunity to ask me questions about the looming crisis. I immediately told him that I thought it was a bad idea and a waste of time. I reasoned that since the civilian employees had the same information as me, and that answers to questions could only come from those further up the chain of command, what value-added information could I provide? Admittedly, I had a selfish motive as well. I truly treasured my lunchtime workout with Ken. He was a trusted colleague, and we often used this exercise time to discuss difficult and complex issues. However, the proposed meetings would interfere with our workout/talk sessions for several days.

Despite my concerns, he talked me into it. However, to prove that I was right and he was wrong, I secretly vowed to keep track of the number of questions that I was able to answer. Given that we were all equally informed and that at my level I had no ability to influence the outcome or provide clarity, I knew I wouldn't be able to provide many answers.

We scheduled three lunchtime meetings over a Monday, Tuesday, and Wednesday in our basement auditorium. On that Monday morning, I entered the stairwell at around 11:55 and, despite being three floors above the auditorium, I could hear the loud discussion emanating up the stairwell. With each step down the stairs, the volume grew. Entering the auditorium, I could feel the nervous anticipation; it blanketed the large, packed room. People were standing in the aisles. All eyes fixed on me, and the room slowly crept to silence.

I started by letting them know that I was there to answer any questions they had regarding the possible government shutdown and furloughs. I shared my concern for them, that I understood their growing apprehension over a host of issues, not the least of which was their personal finances. I made sure to have other key staff members with me to ensure they were given accurate information.

Questions came fast and furious. They ranged from wanting to know the likelihood of the shutdown happening to whether they would eventually get paid in the event they did get furloughed, among a host of others. As predicted, I didn't provide a solid answer to a single question. On Tuesday, we repeated the drill, and the auditorium was about half filled. Again, lots of great questions; I didn't answer any of them.

For the Wednesday meeting, about fifteen employees showed up; a few questions were posed, and none were answered.

I recall walking up the stairwell to my office on that Wednesday afternoon after the last meeting ended. I had a mixture of feelings regarding the meetings. Most revolved around helplessness, frustration, and concern.

There was another feeling that brewed within me: I felt a bit self-righteous. As I had predicted, the meetings were a complete waste of time. Worse yet, I missed three days of exercise, as well as valuable one-on-one time with Ken. I thought of rubbing Ken's nose in it, but I'm glad I resisted. I felt smug and was content with leaving it there. Luckily, a couple weeks later, Congress passed a budget resolution and the government shutdown was avoided.

A few weeks after this averted crisis, it was time for our periodic command climate survey, a confidential commandwide employee engagement tool used by the Department of Defense to assess a host of topics, including organizational effectiveness, equal opportunity, and sexual assault response and prevention. A primary assessment is trust in leadership, and specifically trust in the commanding officer. Respondents can also write comments in the survey. Again, the survey (including all comments) is anonymous. Scores are tabulated for different groups within the command. For example, one can compare the senior officer cohort's level of trust against the junior officer cohort's, or the senior enlisted cohort as compared to the junior enlisted cohort. All cohorts can, of course, be compared to all others.

What level of trust did the civilian employee cohort—the men and women who attended the lunchtime meetings and asked me questions about the potential furlough—have in me? Their level of trust was significantly higher than all other cohorts', and their comments were fascinating. A very common comment was "Captain Brouker spent time with us answering our questions on furloughs!" Reading these, one after another, I thought to myself in amazement, "Who the heck are they talking about? I didn't answer one question!" which was indeed the case.

I can't explain in logical terms what happened here. The fact is over a period of three days I spent about three hours meeting with a large group of employees to address a topic that was of grave concern to them. Never at any time during those three meetings did I provide value-added information; I was not able to provide a solid answer to a single question. Nevertheless, they trusted me significantly more than all other groups in the command, and apparently many within the group perceived that I actually *did* answer their inquiries. In the end, it was obvious that Ken was right and I was wrong: these meetings had clearly not been a waste of time.

What did I learn from this remarkable experience? Simply being there, being visible, and spending time with your team builds trust. You don't need to have all the answers. The truth is you never will. In some cases, like this one, you may not have any answers. However, the team will benefit enormously from your mere presence. We'll talk more in this chapter, as well as later chapters, about the optimal behaviors to employ—and those to avoid—in order to earn trust when you spend time with your team. Suffice to say that your employees want to see your steady hand, confident smile, and calm disposition. This is especially true in times of change, tumult, and uncertainty, which will be discussed in more detail in chapter 10. Being visible is an enormously powerful leadership behavior.

A vexing challenge for every leader at every level is accurately identifying problem areas within their areas of responsibility. The goal, of course, is to know what's going on—to *really* know what's going on. This becomes increasingly difficult as one progresses up the leadership ladder. Having led at a variety of levels, I have experienced this myself. While in command, for example, it took a lot of time and effort to find what I liked to call "the unvarnished truth." Thankfully, before I assumed command, I was warned of this from prior commanding officers. These senior officers advised me that the best way to find out what was really going on was to get out of the office and simply walk around. They gave me wise counsel—they encouraged me to be visible. Always willing to act on wise counsel, I vowed to get out of my office to interact and talk with as many employees as possible.

Such an opportunity presented itself in a unique way on my very first full day in command. On that Monday I decided to go for a jog at noon, which had always been my routine in the Navy. I changed into my gym clothes, ran out the front door of the hospital, and found myself running inside the fence line of the command.[2]

Leadership Lesson

At *all* times, and especially during a crisis, leaders need to get in front of their employees. They want to see a steady hand, a confident smile, and a calm disposition. In person is best, but via webinar works well. You don't need to have all the answers. The truth is you never will.

After a few minutes of running, I saw a young sailor in uniform smoking a cigarette at the smoke pit behind the bachelor enlisted quarters.[3] I approached him, said hello, and asked him how he was doing. He turned to me and said, "Good, how 'bout you?"

I realized by his casual response that he didn't know that I was his commanding officer. Interactions between any officer and enlisted members within the military is extremely formal, with a "sir" or "ma'am" at the beginning or end of the response, or both. Any interaction between the commanding officer and any member within their command—officer or enlisted—is *especially* formal.

The bottom line is that he had no idea who I was. That wasn't surprising. I had taken command just three days prior to this interaction, and not all members of the command—about fifteen hundred people—had attended the ceremony.

In any event, I told him that I was new to the command and asked him how he liked it.

The floodgates opened. He proceeded to tell me, in great detail, all the pros and cons—mostly cons—of being stationed at Naval Hospital Bremerton. Puffing away on his cigarette, needing no prodding on my part, he spewed on and on. To simply say that the intel I got was enlightening would not do it justice. I learned more about the command from that young sailor during our fifteen-minute conversation than I had during the previous weeks when I was given hours of detailed PowerPoint briefings by a host of senior—and sometimes *very* senior—officers.

Navy tradition regarding change of command protocol directs that the outgoing commanding officer spend about four to five working days with the incoming commanding officer to pass along important details of the command. That is exactly what happened in my case—the outgoing commanding officer spent the entire previous week (forty hours or so) providing me with vitally important information on the command. The turnover was thorough, organized, and extremely helpful. As turnovers go, it was very effective. Similarly, prior to assuming command, I spent many days visiting headquarter elements up my chain of command in both San Diego, California, and Washington, D.C. Again, these visits and the information passed on were tremendously helpful. However, the information I received from these hours and days of formal visits and briefings was very different from what I learned in one short conversation with my chain-smoking shipmate at the smoke pit.

About fifteen minutes into our conversation, I casually asked the sailor where he worked at the command.

He told me. Puffing away, he asked, "How 'bout you? Where do you work?"

"Oh, boy," I thought. "Here we go."

"Well . . . I'm your commanding officer."

The sailor almost swallowed his cigarette.

"Sir! Sir! I didn't know . . . sir!" he blurted out between coughs.

I assured my new friend that our conversation had been very informative and useful. I also told him that his insight is exactly what a CO needs to have but doesn't always get. I shared with him my mantra—what I don't know, I can't fix. Even with these reassurances, he still looked very nervous. Before we parted ways, I made sure to thank him earnestly for his thoughts.

Hands shaking a bit, he said, "Thank you, sir. Thank you!"

Over the ensuing weeks and months, I came to learn that everything that sailor told me about the command was 100 percent true.

How can a leader find out what's really going on? Walk around. Be visible.

About midway through my command tour, we were directed to implement an initiative called Patient Centered Medical Home. The program would be far-reaching, as its overall objective was to provide a higher quality of medical care for our patients at a lower cost. One primary objective was to decrease emergency room (ER) visits. In lieu of an ER visit, we wanted our patients to be seen by their assigned primary care provider. While an ER visit provides excellent medical care, the ER provider needs to rapidly become acquainted with the patient's previous history, develop a rapport, and address the patient's presenting problems. The patient also has to quickly come to trust an unfamiliar face. When patients are seen by the same provider, a better standard of care is met. Overall costs are decreased. Not surprisingly, both patients and providers report higher levels of satisfaction. The entire command saw the benefits of this initiative.

To get our Patient Centered Medical Home working, we created a new patient call center. Patients needing a medical appointment were directed to call the center and the call center staff would schedule the appointment with the patient's assigned provider. One key performance indicator that we began tracking immediately was the aggregate number of ER visits over a twenty-four-hour period. Logically, as this initiative took hold, ER visits would decrease.

After its launch, we began tracking ER visits during our board of directors meetings. For the first couple of weeks, we waited patiently for the graph to depict a change in the number of ER visits. However, when the graph remained unchanged after the first month, we became concerned. The fact was, ER visits did not decrease. Everyone, including me, felt a mounting uneasiness during these meetings. After one such meeting, I made a mental note to visit the ER.

Later that day, I visited the ER. It was very busy—screaming babies, phones ringing, staff running back and forth. It was a zoo.

I casually strolled through the waiting area, talking to patients and thanking staff for their work. I introduced myself to one of the staff nurses who looked especially frazzled. I asked her how things were going.

She looked up at me, her head bouncing around, her eyes frowning. "I know who you are. You're the commanding officer." She continued, her voice rising, "If you really want to know how things are going, I'll tell you!"

I didn't need to ask her to continue. She did. "Sir, it's not good!" She looked physically relieved to tell *someone* in authority the truth.

I stayed quiet, letting her continue.

"Here's the deal! Okay . . . you started this Medical Home thing.

The patients have that phone number to call to make their appointments
. . . that call center number. That's *sounds* wonderful, doesn't it?" she said
with swelling sarcasm. "But if you talk to these patients, like I do, lots of
'em will tell you that when they call that number, they're *not* given an
appointment." After another second to catch her breath, she cried with
utter frustration, "Sir, they're being told to go to the ER! This Medical
Home thing is not working!"

"Wow, that's not good!" I thought.

I quickly thanked her, and she went scurrying off.

The next morning, I told the board of directors the story. Later that
day, after some investigating by staff members, it was confirmed that not
all the call center staff had been appropriately trained. Just like the ER
nurse reported, some of these patients were indeed being told to go to
the ER for their care.

After we figured out what had happened, it was an easy fix. We
gave the training to all call center employees, and ER visits began to
decrease.

When you walk around, you can stay informed of the goings-on
throughout the organization; you can find out what's *really* going on.
These personal interactions are also golden opportunities to speak with
staff members in their own work spaces, which makes them much more
comfortable speaking openly. You'll appear more engaged and approachable. When employees have a good relationship with their boss, they're
much more willing to provide valuable input. Decision making is optimized—better decisions are made because the decision makers are better
informed—and team performance is maximized. Absent this relationship, employees will be less willing to be forthcoming with ideas and
suggestions for improvement.

Leadership Lesson

Be visible. Be approachable. You can connect personally with people at every level, drive out fear, and create trust. Subordinates
will be more comfortable speaking their mind, and decision making will be optimized.

Like any behavior, there can be pitfalls with this one. Here's one you'll want to avoid: don't treat this like an aimless activity. Be strategic; proactively schedule time to walk around. More importantly, try to visit each area with the same periodicity, what I like to call "spreading the wealth." For example, maybe set a goal to visit each team once a week. It's easy to get into a routine and visit the same group of people at the expense of others. That could be perceived as favoritism, and that causes problems. Visit all departments, no matter their role (i.e., mail room, custodial volunteers, etc.). Take the time to briefly explain how their role impacts the mission. This concept similarly applies when attending social events—make sure to "spread the wealth" at these events. To avoid the perception of favoritism, your objective at social events is to, if possible, briefly visit with each and every attendee.

My best day in command was spent wandering around the hospital complex the entire day. After the morning board of directors meeting, I'd head out and wander the command, interacting with the sailors and employees. I loved it for many reasons—I was able to thank them for their efforts, ask them how I could help, and banter with them about topics I knew were of interest to them (sports, hobbies, family). I was also able to get a good feel for the morale within the command. However, my "wanderings" were not random events. They often had a purpose.

For example, during our board of directors meeting every morning, I found it valuable to carefully watch the reactions of the different board members as issues were deliberated. The members had healthy disagreements over issues and respectfully voiced their concerns during our meetings. However, despite working diligently to reduce tension among this important body, I understood that not everyone was always going to speak their mind.

This was generally more prevalent with newer members of the board. They were less inclined to risk speaking their mind for fear of alienating themselves from the group. Once in a while, I sensed that even seasoned board members would sometimes elect to keep their thoughts to themselves. Perhaps they weren't convinced their point was important, or maybe the meeting was simply running late.

Regardless, I would watch members' body language. If I sensed that they had something to contribute but weren't speaking up, I'd either ask them for their thoughts then and there or make a mental note to visit them in their work space some time during the day.

I found that visiting them in *their* work space was an especially valuable use of time. After casually exchanging pleasantries, I'd ask them their thoughts on the issue. I don't recall a time when these conversations didn't produce valuable information. Because I had more accurate information, we made better decisions on a number of issues.

Invariably, these informal visits were more productive than a formal meeting. Under these circumstances, an employee can feel less inhibited about sharing thoughts, ideas, and concerns without being scrutinized by their peers. The nature of the visit is made less formal due to it being held on their "turf" versus being called to the boss's office. Finally, by casually visiting, trading small talk and avoiding a scheduled meeting, barriers are brought down and a more inviting atmosphere is created.

Getting out of the office, being visible, and visiting with your employees is time-consuming. No question. However, when you understand and appreciate the impact that a face-to-face interaction has on building trust, you'll begin to recognize these as wise investments of your time. It is time extremely well spent.

The great leaders fully appreciate that all interactions between themselves and their employees are opportunities to further build on their relationship—that these interactions can increase the employee's sense of well-being and give them more confidence in their leader. As such, great leaders create *more* of these interactions. They proactively schedule time to get out of their office to increase their visibility and, consequently, more effectively leverage this powerful behavior.

When I ask my seminar participants to list attributes of great leaders whom they loved working for, a very common answer is "being approachable." I've given my seminars in many countries and talked with diverse audiences. Regardless of country or cultural makeup, they always identify "being approachable" as a top attribute of a great leader. People love working with leaders they feel comfortable being around.

When done correctly, being visible helps the boss become more approachable. The key words here are "when done correctly." Not all leaders who make themselves visible become approachable. As with the "proactively know your staff" behavior, while there is much to gain by being visible, there are some pitfalls to watch out for.

This was clearly illustrated by one of the commanding officers who worked for me during my chief of staff, Navy Medicine West tour. Before a new CO would assume command of their hospital, they would spend a few days with Navy Medicine West staff learning unique aspects of their command and building relationships with key staff members. Each new CO would spend some time with me. We'd spend the first thirty minutes getting to know one another, and then we'd talk about leadership and I'd briefly touch on every leadership behavior discussed in this book. Included in the discussion, of course, was the importance of being visible.

One of the first COs who went through this process was a highly talented, extremely intelligent officer named Sid. Sid and I had worked together previously. I knew him well, and we had gotten along great. He had an excellent service reputation and was excited to take command.

Sid was a quiet and introverted person. When we discussed the importance of being visible, we openly discussed how this behavior was generally easier for extroverted leaders. While he fully acknowledged that getting out and walking around the command would be more challenging for him, he appreciated its importance. Sid was fully on board with the concept and was committed to being a visible CO.

Every two weeks, I would conduct one-on-one mentoring meetings via phone with all first-year commanding officers. During my calls with Sid, I would often ask if he had been able to get out of his office and walk around the hospital. He would always enthusiastically reply that he had. He reported that while it continued to be a bit of an effort, walking around was becoming less onerous. I was very heartened to hear this and encouraged him to continue.

About six months into Sid's command tour, four members of the admiral's staff, including myself, visited Sid's hospital. The other two members of the admiral's team included a senior non-commissioned officer (command master chief, Navy Medicine West) and the admiral's aide. It was a routine visit—the admiral visited each of the ten hospitals within Navy Medicine West at least annually.

At around 7:00 a.m. on the first day of the visit, the admiral met with the three of us to review the day's schedule. The first official meeting was scheduled to start at 0800 and run for several hours—the admiral and I were to be briefed on a variety of metrics by members of Sid's board of directors. While the admiral and I fully understood the importance of these meetings, we both much preferred to simply walk around the command and meet the people working there. That part of the visit was scheduled for the afternoon.

It was decided—to their great relief—that the other two members of the admiral's staff (his aide and the command master chief) would not attend the 0800 meeting. The admiral's aide would catch up on correspondence, and the master chief would walk around the command and talk with sailors and staff to get a measure of staff morale. Senior non-commissioned officers, Navy chiefs, are excellent at this task. Master chiefs, at the top of the chief food chain, are the absolute best.

Only twenty minutes into the morning meeting with the board of directors, out of the corner of my eye I saw the master chief open the door at the back of the conference room and quietly walk in. He silently walked over to me and whispered, "Sir, we need to talk."

"This can't be good," I thought as we walked toward the door.

Leaving the conference room and entering the hallway, he looked around to ensure no one was around. Seeing that we were alone, he said, "Sir, we've got a problem!"

"What's up, master chief?" I asked, trying to hide my rising concern.

"We've got a problem, sir. Oh yeah, we've got a problem!" he repeated with mounting excitement.

He continued, "You know how you keep tellin' all these COs to be more visible? You know . . . walk around. Oh, this CO's walking around . . . he's walking around all right! Do you know what he's saying when he's walking around?"

"No. What's he saying?" I asked with growing unease.

"Well, he's walking around with that big ol' command pin asking people, 'What's my mission, vision, and guiding principles?'[4] That's all he's talking to them about. It's not good, sir!"

Getting more animated, he said, "No one knows that shit, sir. People see him coming and they're running like rats off a sinking ship! It's not good, sir. It's not good!"

Holy smokes! I realized that while I had told Sid to walk around, I didn't tell him that these were to be informal and relaxed visits.

"Sir, please, for the sake of my sailors, sir, you need to take care of this!" he pleaded.

One needs to appreciate the enormous authority bestowed on a U.S. military commanding officer—the title is very appropriate. As mentioned, while all leaders are naturally intimidating by the very fact that they exert influence over others, a commanding officer of a military unit can be *very* intimidating.

I immediately envisioned the staff at Sid's hospital seeing Sid innocently approach from a distance. The savvy ones—those who were plugged in and aware of the "what's my mission, vision, and guiding principles" questions that were coming from the commanding officer—would find something, anything, to do. How busy they'd suddenly become! They'd scatter. The only staff members left behind for Sid to talk with were the more naïve, less informed ones—the young sailors who'd maybe been on board only a few days or weeks and hadn't gotten the word to scatter when Sid was coming. The interaction probably didn't end well.

That evening, after a very long day of briefings and meetings, I visited Sid in his office. As a prior CO, I remembered how emotionally and physically exhausted I was after these visits from headquarters. I was always glad when they were over, and I was sure Sid felt the same way. I was sympathetic that Sid was glad that our visit was behind him.

As I entered Sid's office, I found him slumped at his desk reading emails. He looked beat. After some small talk about the visit, I asked, "Hey, Sid, when you're walking around the hospital, what're you talking to the staff about?"

Wearily he said, "Oh, we're talking about mission and vision . . . you know, that stuff."

Like employees at any organization, sailors enjoy talking about a host of topics; however, very rarely are mission and vision on that list.

I said with a smile, "Sid, come on, man. I've never met a sailor who voluntarily started talking about that stuff. Have you? Who's initiating the topic?"

"Well, I guess I am," he said, still not understanding where this conversation was going.

Still smiling, I said, "Think about this for a second. If the admiral came in here right now and asked you to recite his mission, vision, and guiding principles, what would you do?"

Instantly Sid's face contorted into a look of horror. He understood immediately: he was intimidating his staff by asking these questions.

Sid asked apologetically, "Wow, what should I do?"

I immediately responded, "Just stop doing it. Instead of talking about that stuff, simply thank them for what they do at your command and ask them if there is anything you can do to help."

Sid was very appreciative and vowed to change his ways. The good news is that he did. After a period of time, he was welcomed by his staff during his visits and successfully completed his command tour.

Being visible is a double-edged sword. Not all leaders who make themselves visible become approachable. The key is how the leader behaves. During each and every interaction with employees, it is the leader's behavior that will dictate whether the leader becomes approachable or not. All leaders fall on a dynamic spectrum between the two extremes of "approachable" and "intimidating." Where they fall on this spectrum can change frequently, all dictated by the leader's behaviors during interactions; the leader's perceived level of either approachability or intimidation will move accordingly.

Approachable leaders are better-informed leaders, and better-informed leaders will make better decisions.

"Knowing your staff" and "being visible" are two behaviors that work hand in hand. Recall from the last chapter that by taking notes during the "getting to know you" meeting, you'll be better able to recall a few important facts about your employee—maybe a hobby, a goal, or a challenge that they're facing. If you cross paths with them while walking around, you can ask them about it. Do *not* underestimate the impact of this type of interaction. When you pass an employee in the hallway and refer to a topic that they mentioned during the "get to know you" one-on-one meeting, that's very powerful. You listened. You remembered. You care. An otherwise ordinary moment is transformed into an extremely powerful one. Let me close this chapter with a story that demonstrates how "knowing your staff" and "being visible" are two behaviors that work extremely well together.

Leadership Lesson

- Proactively schedule time to walk around.
- This is not an aimless activity. Ensure that you "spread the wealth"—visit each area with the same periodicity. For example, maybe visit each team once a week.
- Spread the wealth when attending social events. Your goal is to briefly visit with each and every member of your team in attendance.
- Being visible is a double-edged sword. The leader's specific behaviors while in the presence of employees will dictate the culture. An intimidating leader will create a environment of fear. An approachable leader will create a environment of trust.

Walking around do's and don'ts:

Do:

- Be honest if asked a question. It's OK if you don't know the answer.
- Give thanks.
- Give accolades—celebrate the hundreds of small successes.
- Ask, "What can I do to help you?"
- Connect the dots; explain the why.
- Show a steady hand, a confident smile, and a calm disposition.
- Smile.

Don't:

- Pretend to know all the answers.
- Test employees with pop questions, such as reciting company-wide guiding principles.
- Discuss poor performance.
- Talk too much. No one is going to tell the boss to stop talking.
- Constantly frown.

During my last month of duty as XO at the Naval Hospital in Rota, Spain, I was informed that a sailor was requesting to see me. While there was no additional information provided regarding the reason for her request, I was informed that she considered it important that we meet before I left Rota. Indeed, I was scheduled to detach Rota the following month to begin my command tour in Bremerton, Washington.

I did not recall her name when told of her request. My staff informed me that she had done a very good job at the command. She was a stellar performer. In fact, she had helped with many volunteer events, and she certainly hadn't gotten into any trouble so far during her tour. I had no other information regarding the reason for her request to meet with me.

My initial thoughts were not pleasant ones. While any sailor can request a meeting with either the XO or the CO, it's not a common event. In my experience, the sailor usually has a grievance or a significant problem.

After exchanging pleasantries, I asked her how I could help her and braced myself. She started by saying that she was aware that I was moving shortly to my new assignment as CO at Naval Hospital Bremerton and that the job would be a very busy one.

Still bracing myself, I smiled and nodded.

She went on to say, "You probably don't recall when we met after I arrived at the command. It was right here in this office. You asked me to tell you my story."

I had hundreds of "tell me your story" conversations with sailors and employees. I did not recall this one. I continued to listen with increasing interest.

She continued, "While telling you my story, I mentioned that my big concern was day care for my child. I am a single mom and hadn't yet figured out day care for my daughter. After the meeting you introduced me to the command master chief, Master Chief Crawford, who was extremely helpful. She put me in touch with the right people, and my day care issue was fixed."

"That's great to hear. It doesn't surprise me. Master Chief Crawford has helped many sailors with tough issues," I said, thinking of the many times she had indeed helped others in their time of need.

She continued, "I also want to tell you what happened a couple of days after our initial meeting. You were walking around in my work space, visiting and talking with my colleagues. When you saw me, you quietly asked me about my daughter and if I had found day care."

She paused. Appearing to fight back tears, she said, "Sir, I'll never forget that. It showed that the command *really* cared."

After a couple of seconds, she regained her composure and continued. "Sir, I know you're leaving soon. I wanted to tell you that this incident had a profound impact on me. I *knew* this command would take care of my daughter and me. You cannot imagine the sense of relief I felt."

She continued, "I'm telling you this to encourage you to do the same thing in Bremerton. Get to know your people and walk around. I know you'll be very busy in that job. But sir, you *must* find the time."

Although that conversation took place many years ago, I'll never forget its impact on me—I received validation of its immense impact when this sailor told me this story.

Proactively getting to know your employees and spending time with them are powerful leadership behaviors. When used in tandem, their power can be exponential. When you know your staff, you know something about them that you can refer to when you're walking around. Both behaviors will strengthen your relationships and help build more trust up and down the chain of command.

KEY POINTS

1. At *all* times, and especially during a crisis, leaders need to get in front of their employees. They want to see a steady hand, a confident smile, and a calm disposition. In person is best, but via webinar works well. You don't need to have all the answers. The truth is you never will.
2. Be visible. Be approachable. You can connect personally with people at every level, drive out fear, and create trust. Subordinates will be more comfortable speaking their mind, and decision making will be optimized.

3. Action items for optimizing the "being visible" behavior:

- Proactively schedule time to walk around.
- This is not an aimless activity. Ensure that you "spread the wealth." Your goal is to visit each area with the same periodicity. For example, maybe visit each team once a week.
- Spread the wealth when attending social events. Your goal is to briefly visit with each and every member of your team in attendance.
- Being visible is a double-edged sword. The leader's specific behaviors while in the presence of employees will dictate the culture. An intimidating leader will create a environment of fear. An approachable leader will create a environment of trust.

Walking around do's and don'ts:

Do:

- Be honest if asked a question. It's OK if you don't know the answer.
- Give thanks.
- Give accolades—celebrate the hundreds of small successes.
- Ask, "What can I do to help you?"
- Connect the dots; explain the why.
- Show a steady hand, a confident smile, and a calm disposition.
- Smile.

Don't:

- Pretend to know all the answers.
- Test employees with pop questions, such as reciting company-wide guiding principles.
- Discuss poor performance.
- Talk too much. No one is going to tell the boss to stop talking.
- Constantly frown.

6

RESPECT

Lincoln treated all people, including his rivals, with dignity and respect and found a path to friendship with each of them . . . and it paid enormous dividends over time.

—Doris Kearns Goodwin,
Team of Rivals: The Political Genius of Abraham Lincoln

A large survey was recently conducted that included twenty thousand employees working in a variety of industries around the world.[1] The survey asked a simple question: What was the most important leadership behavior for garnering commitment and engagement?

Participants were given the following five choices:

1. Inspiring vision
2. Providing useful feedback
3. Recognition and appreciation
4. Being treated with respect
5. Opportunities for learning, growth, and development

All leaders would agree all five are important. However, one was the overwhelming choice. Which one? It may surprise you. The answer: "Being treated with respect." In fact, the authors concluded, "There's one thing that leaders need to demonstrate: respect. No other leadership behavior had a bigger effect on employees."

Recall that the culture of any team is on a very dynamic spectrum between trust and fear. The continual movement on this spectrum is determined by the leader's behaviors during these hundreds of interac-

---

Leadership Lesson

Leaders need to show respect toward their employees. Respect impacts employee engagement more than any other leadership behavior.

---

tions on a day-to-day, hour-to-hour, minute-to-minute, and second-to-second basis. The leader *owns* the culture.

This survey, and many others with similar findings, strongly suggests that the leader's level of respect toward employees during these interactions has a *significant* impact on the environment that is created. Taking care of your staff by showing them respect increases commitment and engagement.

It's much easier to treat others with respect and, frankly, more fun to be a leader when all is going well. As a leader, I especially loved Fridays—even more so on a Friday before a three-day weekend. People were in good moods. Morale was high. Conversations about weekend plans were light and airy. Treating people with respect on Fridays was much easier than, say, on Mondays. For me, it seemed more times than not that bad news came on a Monday.

As a leader, you're *guaranteed* one thing: challenges, issues, and problems are coming your way. Getting bad news and facing adversity is a certainty—it's not a matter of if but when. These are gut-wrenching experiences that mold you as a leader. Getting bad news—and, more accurately, how you *react* to that bad news—has a significant impact on the culture you create—again, a culture that you own. While we cannot control the fact that we're going to get bad news, we can certainly control our behavior when it comes. If you remain respectful and maintain your composure, not only will your employees have more confidence in you as a leader, but your calmness will also spread to them—which will optimize decision making. If you show anger or, worse yet, shoot the messenger, you'll lose the respect of your employees, and your unease will likewise infect others—all of which will hamper decision making.

These are crucible moments for a leader. Great leaders are mindful of their impact on others during crises and monitor or become even more intentional during their interactions. They appreciate these moments as tremendous opportunities to bring calm out of chaos. Leaders who remain calm, collected, compassionate, and respectful when the tempest comes garner trust and spread confidence. Great leaders remain respectful when the team is in troubled waters. While it's easy to be respectful when all is going well, the test will come when adversity strikes. (We'll talk more about leading during a crises in chapter 10.)

Midway through my Navy career, I was working at a naval hospital as a senior member of the governing board of directors. My boss at that time had an unfortunate habit of getting angry over any and all kinds of bad news. Any hint of bad news and boom: anger! The only upside was that the reaction was very consistent—he always shot the messenger. The only variable was how much anger would be exerted during the shooting. Unfortunately, I was usually the messenger being shot. His rude, unpleasant, and unprofessional behavior was disrespectful and showed a gross lack of regard for others. It disturbed everyone, and many people were afraid of him. Not surprisingly, the culture at that hospital was one of fear.

One such incident occurred when I had about three months left at this duty station. The hospital was preparing for a combination of two comprehensive inspections that are routinely conducted every three years at all Navy Medicine commands worldwide. The Joint Commission Accreditation[2] and Navy Medical Inspector General[3] teams would soon be visiting and inspecting our command. In addition to ensuring we were compliant with hundreds of clinical and administrative items, we also wanted all areas to be clean, tidy, and inspection ready. It is typically a period of time that generates increased tension. As part of our preparation, I had officers who worked for me inspect different areas of

---

Leadership Lesson

Times of chaos, tumult, and uncertainty are tremendous opportunities for a leader to positively impact team culture.

the hospital. During one of these routine inspections, something very bizarre was discovered.

I was in my office late on a Thursday evening answering emails when Lieutenant (LT) King, one of the inspecting officers, entered my office to brief me on the inspection he had conducted that day.[4] One of the buildings LT King had inspected was the blood bank. Like all hospitals, we had a refrigerated blood bank that stored blood and fresh frozen plasma.

After exchanging some pleasantries, he said, "Well, sir, I inspected the blood bank and cleaned it up a bit, sir. It looks good sir, I . . . uh . . . I moved some boxes around and . . . uh . . . again, all squared away, sir."

"That's great." It all sounded pretty routine.

LT King began nervously pacing back and forth in front of my desk. "Thanks, sir . . . thanks. Uh, one other thing, sir," he said, his pace accelerating. "When I was inspecting the freezer where the plasma was stored, I moved some boxes around . . . and . . . I found . . . ah . . . I found a leg."

His statement jolting me, I asked, "A *what*? Did you say *leg*? What kind of leg?"

I hoped desperately that he'd say I'd misheard him, but talking faster and a bit louder, he responded, "Yes, sir . . . yes, sir . . . a leg . . a human leg, sir! It looks like a below-the-knee amputation, sir!"

Talking much faster, almost rambling, he continued, "Yes, sir, it was behind some boxes. A human leg . . . frozen solid! It had a tag attached to the big toe . . . looked like the last four digits of a social security number and a date. It seems like it's been there quite a while, sir. Almost five years, sir!"

He continued, more or less repeating the story. I tried to listen, but my mind raced with a number of fleeting thoughts.

My immediate thought involved cascading memories of all the tremendous leadership development training that the Navy had sent me to over the past twenty or so years. Ample training—an abundance of training. I mused that I must have missed the class on what you're to do when you find a human body part in a building!

My mind continued to race. Next I had a bit of a pity party.

Feeling sorry for myself, I thought of how that damn leg had been in that building for five years. Why did it have to turn up now, on *my* watch, at *this* time, a few weeks before a major inspection? It could have remained in there another three short months and my replacement would've had to deal with it. It was found—now *I* had to deal with it.

Then came a very troubling thought—one that quickly consumed me. I realized that I'd have to tell the boss the next morning, and that would be ugly. This was, of course, not good news. I envisioned the scene with the boss, and it wasn't a pleasant one.

Recovering from my racing thoughts, I cleared my head and refocused on LT King.

Everyone at the command was aware of the boss's anger issue, including of course LT King. No words needed to be spoken between us, but one nightmarish thought we both shared was of the boss's angry reaction to this news.

Very quietly and slowly, LT King whispered, "Sir, one other thing. We can get rid of the leg . . . *tonight!*"

My curiosity piqued, I asked in a subdued voice, "What do you mean get rid of the leg?"

Talking much faster, he confidently stated, "Sir, we have a contract with a local incineration company. I'm the facilities manager and know all about that contract. I'm always calling them up, usually after hours, to come to the hospital with a truck to pick up cardboard boxes. They routinely haul the boxes away and burn 'em at their facility."

He continued, talking quieter and slower, almost pleading, "Sir, I'll call them tonight and tell them we have some boxes to burn. I'll collect some boxes. They'll take the boxes. They'll burn the boxes."

He continued in a whisper, "Except *tonight*, sir, I'll slip the leg in one of the boxes. You and I are the only ones who know about the leg. Easy day, sir."

"That sounds simple enough," I thought. "I won't have to deal with telling the boss and we're done. Perfect."

I shook my head, trying to forget about the whole mess. Fortunately, I slowed my thoughts down. I looked up and said, "It's late. I'm tired." Recalling some mentor in my past warning me not to make decisions when tired, I said, "How long did you say the leg's been in there?"

"Five years, sir . . . looks like five years."

What to do? I glanced at the mounting pile of folders in my inbox.

I had a lot of stuff on my plate. Now this leg mess! I suddenly felt overwhelmed and exhausted.

Trying desperately to maintain my composure, I said, "Okay, here's the deal. The leg's been in there five years . . . it can stay in there one more night. I need to sleep on this."

As LT King was leaving my office, he tried one more desperate appeal: "Okay, sir. Got it. Just let me know if you change your mind . . . if you want me to take care of it, you know, tonight. All you have to do is call me. You have my cell number, sir." I think I saw him wink as he closed the door behind him.

Alone in my office. What to do? I looked again at my inbox and groaned. I decided that I'd had enough that day and headed for home.

As I drove home, thoughts of the leg consumed me. I smiled, thinking how easy it would be to simply burn that stupid leg! I glanced at my cell phone sitting on the passenger seat a few times as I drove. One quick phone call to LT King and issue resolved. Leg gone. I just *did not* want to deal with telling the boss the next morning.

My wife, Kris, has always been my trusted confidante. As soon as I saw her, I told her of the whole leg mess.

She asked me, with some suspicion, "You aren't seriously thinking of burning that leg . . . are you?"

"Well . . ." I sheepishly began to answer.

Before I could continue, she emphatically said, "You can't burn that leg! You need to tell the boss the truth. A coverup is always worse than dealing with the truth. You need to tell him first thing tomorrow morning."

Her comments jolted me back to clearer thinking. She was absolutely right—I needed to tell the boss. I was embarrassed that I had even contemplated burning the leg. I knew in my heart what the right thing to do was: tell the boss. Even though this occurred many years ago, I still find it striking that I even contemplated burning that leg.

While I found comfort in finally deciding to do the right thing, I was still worried about the boss's reaction the next morning when I dropped the news. That night, I tossed and turned in a fitful sleep. I tried to understand how this could have happened. I anguished as I anticipated the hard questions that I had no answers for. After a horrible night of worried wakefulness, I braced myself for the carnage that was to come.

I told the boss first thing that morning. It was ugly.

I hate to admit it, but I was pretty ineffective the rest of that Friday. I found it difficult to focus. I had lost some of my confidence. A simple task that would have normally taken me minutes to accomplish took me much longer. I was distracted and clearly not on my game.

My effectiveness was diminished not only on that Friday but well into the weekend. Even though I was with my family that weekend, I continued to ruminate on the whole mess. It bothered me.

On the following Monday morning, the boss and I conversed about a host of issues, including, of course, the leg. The conversation went well. We calmly agreed to conduct a fully transparent investigation to try to solve the leg mystery.[5] Thankfully, there were no angry outbursts from the boss.

I tell this story at many of my leadership seminars. After one such seminar, a gentleman approached me during a break and told me that he was a pathologist and had been practicing for many years. He mentioned that he loved the leg story and went on to inform me that, while it is relatively uncommon to lose body parts in his line of work, it indeed happens.

I vividly remember him asking me point-blank, "What was the big deal?"

I immediately thought, "What's the big deal . . . what's the big deal . . . are you kidding me? The big deal is that we'd found a leg that had been sitting around in a freezer for five years!"

Seeing my facial expression and probably reading my thoughts, he said that he didn't want to sound gruesome, but again, in his years of experience, body parts are sometimes lost. While very rare, it happens. When it does, they investigate and learn from the incident. It's really not a big deal.

I thought about it—why *was* this such a big deal? Then it hit me: It was a big deal because of the culture—specifically, the culture of fear that permeated the organization. Morale was low. Creativity was crushed, and staff were focused solely on day-to-day tasks. Following rules and avoiding blame were top priorities. Collaborating, experimenting, and having fun were absent. People were reluctant to speak up, and the omnipresent fear was *never* discussed—it was the elephant in the room.

My pathologist friend then asked me a thought-provoking question:

"What would you have done if the same incident occurred while you were working for a boss that you loved working for?"

Thinking about that gave me an immediate revelation. I instantly thought of the last boss I had in my Navy career. He was Admiral Forrest Faison, and he was Commander, Navy Medicine West (NMW). He was responsible for ten hospitals spanning the West Coast to the Indian Ocean and health care for eight hundred thousand patients. We had fifteen thousand employees working for us. I was his chief of staff, equivalent to chief operating officer for NMW.

Given that span of control, during the two years I was chief of staff, you can imagine the number of times I had to break bad news to him. Many of these calls involved more shocking news than a missing leg. On my first day on the job, Admiral Faison informed me that bad news does not get better with time. The message was clear: Don't sit on bad news. He wanted to be informed sooner rather than later. It should be noted that the hospitals in our region were located in numerous time zones. As such, phone calls to the boss often occurred well after normal working hours. Regardless of how bizarre the news was, or when it was delivered, he *never* got angry. He was *always* respectful. In fact, it seemed the more outrageous the story, the calmer he reacted.

I reflected that if Admiral Faison were my boss during the leg incident, I would have immediately picked up the phone and started the conversation with "Sir, you're not going to believe this, but . . ."

After hearing of the leg discovered behind boxes in the fresh frozen plasma freezer, he would have responded with "Wow, I thought I've heard everything, but that's a new one for me!"

He'd continue with his go-to comment: "Well, Mark, let me know what you find out. Thanks."

That's it. *"Well, Mark, let me know what you find out."* No anger. No outrage.

We would have initiated the same root cause analysis investigation that we ultimately conducted. We would have uncovered the same results. We would have passed the inspections. However, under Admiral Faison, I would not have gotten distracted and lost focus, sleep, or time. I certainly would not have courted ill-advised plans—like burning the leg! An environment of fear breeds unwise plans.

While Admiral Faison was talented in many areas, what set him apart from other leaders whom I worked for was his ability to *always* remain calm, collected, compassionate, and respectful. He always brought order out of chaos and uncertainty. Consequently, despite his high rank, he was very approachable. We all trusted him and worked hard for him, and our confidence, focus, well-being, and overall performance excelled under his leadership. Our region consistently far exceeded all annual quality and workload goals and led the other two Navy Medicine regions in nearly all key performance indicators. Not surprisingly, Admiral Faison became the Navy's thirty-eighth surgeon general. What was the key to our success under his leadership? Trust.

Recall the data from the Gallup study presented in chapter 2. A total of twenty-eight thousand employees responded to a survey that measured employee engagement. Scores were compiled such that the seventy-five stores with the highest employee engagement scores were identified as a cohort as well as the seventy-five stores with the lowest scores. Profits were then ascertained for each cohort. The high-engagement stores exceeded their annualized profit goals by an average of 14 percent, while the low-engagement stores missed their profit goals by a full 30 percent.

Likewise, the study conducted by the Great Place to Work Institute revealed that over an eighteen-year period, the one hundred companies that were selected as great places to work achieved annualized stock returns that were nearly three times the market average.

How does one explain these study results? Leaders whose behaviors create a culture of trust enjoy lower staff turnover, more job applicants, and lower absenteeism. There are fewer disruptions and distractions, as

---

Leadership Lesson

- When bad news comes, take a breath, thank the messenger, and ask the messenger to thank whoever told them.
- Under *no* circumstance should you shoot the messenger.
- Remember: This is your crucible moment. How you choose to behave at this moment greatly impacts team culture.

well as less overall stress, and employees are able to focus on the job at hand. A pleasant workplace environment enhances team performance.

On a much deeper level, researchers have shown that when leaders build strong relationships and create a caring culture, a response is triggered at the neurotransmitter level among team members. Amazingly, oxytocin is released from the brain of these team members in response to the positive social interaction initiated by the boss.[6] Oxytocin is a molecule that is also known as the "love hormone"—it is released from the brain as a result of social bonding. For example, oxytocin levels increase when two people hug. Higher levels of oxytocin have been shown to increase empathy, engagement, trust, and cooperation, as well as forgiveness.[7] These researchers have shown that when leaders lead with care and compassion through positive social interactions, oxytocin levels increase among team members, as does their overall performance.

In a culture of fear, the opposite is true. With fear comes high absenteeism, more disruptions, distractions, and stress. Researchers have found that people working under these conditions also undergo changes at the neurotransmitter level. Modern science has much to tell us about what happens under these circumstances. When workers experience intermittent workplace stressors—like being on the receiving end of an angry outburst for too long or too often—they'll have higher cortisol levels circulating in their bodies, which causes significant health problems.[8] Cortisol is the body's primary chronic-stress chemical and, when raised for extended periods of time, can deplete your immune system, causing cardiovascular disease, cancer, diabetes, and ulcers.[9] Indeed, researchers have shown that working in a group where incivility is present adversely affects workers' mental health.[10] Another study followed eight hundred workers from a variety of professions over a twenty-year period. They interviewed these adults repeatedly about work conditions, their boss's behavior, and collaboration among their colleagues—all while closely monitoring the participants' health. The presence of less kind colleagues was associated with a much higher risk of dying.[11] Researchers have also found that people not only carry this stress with them while at work but also tend to take the stress of abrasive behavior home with them, unleashing it on family members.[12]

When a worker is on the receiving end of an angry outburst for too long or too often, not only is their health impacted, but so is their performance. In a poll of eight hundred managers and employees across seventeen industries, researchers found that among workers who have been on the receiving end of rude behavior, 80 percent lost work time worrying about the incident, 78 percent said that their commitment to the organization declined, 63 percent lost time avoiding the offender, and 48 percent decreased their work effort, among other alarming findings.[13]

Because the behaviors of the leader are generally emulated, when the boss acts rude and disrespectful, it is more likely that others in the organization will also act this way. These subtle (and maybe not so subtle) acts of disrespect ripple down the chain of command, and the organization moves toward a culture of fear—a culture in which people are much more reluctant to tell the truth and divulge bad news. A state of blissful ignorance is no place for a leader—disaster awaits the ill-informed boss. In the end, cultures of fear are breeding ground for unwise decisions. Going back to the leg story, I courted a potentially disastrous course of action—burning the leg—because of a leader who led with anger. He had a well-deserved reputation for shooting the messenger.

Leaders need to be told the bad news. They need the truth, however ugly that may be. A leader can't fix things of which they're unaware. Getting bad news comes with being a leader—it's not a matter of *if*, but rather *when*. While you can't control the bad news, you can control your reaction when it comes. We don't have do-overs. Whatever we say, whatever we do, however we react, we can't take it back. We have one chance to get it right.

What about mild incivility? Does even mild incivility impact team performance? Researchers conducted a fascinating study to find out.[14] They explored the impact of rudeness on the performance of medical teams.

Twenty-four neonatal intensive care unit (NICU) teams, each composed of one physician and two nurses, participated in a training exercise (simulation) involving an infant (a preterm medical mannequin) who was suffering from necrotizing enterocolitis (NEC).[15] None of the teams were told that the mannequin was suffering from NEC; each team was to correctly diagnose NEC and then select and perform the proper treatment. The simulation for all twenty-four teams was recorded. Three independent NICU staff (two senior physicians and one senior nurse) reviewed the recordings and rated each team's performance regarding their ability to correctly diagnose and treat.

Prior to the simulation, all twenty-four teams were informed that a foreign expert on team dynamics and team adaptability in medicine would observe them. Teams were randomly exposed to either "mild rudeness" (thirteen teams) or "no rudeness" (eleven teams). What incivility were participants in the "mild rudeness" cohort exposed to? The foreign expert told these teams that he had already observed a number of groups from hospitals in their country and was "not impressed with the quality of medicine and that he hoped that he would not get sick during his visit." The other cohort of teams—the control group or "no rudeness"—were simply told by the foreign observer that he "hoped we would all learn from the workshop."

What did they find? Was there a difference in performance between the two cohorts? The cohort exposed to rudeness prior to the simulation were significantly less likely to correctly diagnose and treat than the cohort not exposed to rudeness. Researchers found that rudeness reduced information sharing among the team members. This, in turn, hampered their ability to correctly diagnose NEC. Similarly, those in the cohort exposed to rudeness were less likely to ask for help from their team members, which hindered their ability to correctly treat the NEC. For example, if one member of the three-member team needed help properly ventilating the patient, those exposed to rudeness were less likely to ask another team member for assistance, while those not exposed to rudeness were more likely to ask for that assistance; in other words, those not exposed to rudness worked better as a team.

The authors concluded that even mild incivility common in medical practice can have "profound, if not devastating, effects on patient care." That's a powerful statement, but it correctly reflects the results of this well-designed study. In other words, this study found that even subtle and seemingly benign aggression—mild incivility—negatively impacts team performance. The authors also conclude that leaders should spend more time paying close attention to *how* they behave during interactions with their staff.

Why does disrespectful behavior have such a profound impact on team performance? Psychologists have discovered that disrespectful behavior hinders working memory.[16] Working memory is used to temporarily store and manage the information required for people to carry out complex tasks such as learning, reasoning, and understanding. Working memory is important for reasoning and guides our decision making and behavior. This is where most planning, analysis, and management of goals occurs. In other words, disrespectful behavior impedes team performance because it hinders one's ability to learn, reason, comprehend, plan, and analyze. The bottom line is this: When the bad news comes, it is imperative that leaders maintain their composure. Better yet, instead of getting angry, thank them for bringing the news to you, and instruct them to thank whoever told them.

As you become more mindful of the impact that interactions have on culture, remember a common pitfall of these interactions: no one is going to tell the boss to stop talking. While you're conversing with an employee, be careful not to dominate the conversation. Being mindful of your subordinate's valuable time is an excellent opportunity to demonstrate respect. However, dominating the conversation is an easy pitfall for leaders to fall into. Why? Again, it's a rare employee who will tell the boss to stop talking. Remember the premise that along with the title of leader comes a level of intimidation? Routinely monopolizing a discussion or conversation reinforces that tenet.

One of the more arduous tours of duty I had in the Navy was a job that required sixty-plus hours per week. I knew going in that it would require that level of effort—it simply came with the territory. I girded myself for a demanding tour. Despite the long hours, I knew this would help me grow as a leader, and I was very excited for the opportunity.

At that time, we still had children in high school and middle school.

Leadership Lesson

A culture of fear breeds unwise decisions. A precursor to a culture of fear—disrespectful behavior—impedes team performance by hindering one's ability to learn, reason, comprehend, plan, and analyze.

I've always been mindful of my work-life balance. However, I knew this tour was going to be a challenge and vowed to be careful not to neglect my family.

What I did not factor into my time management equation was a boss who would enter my work space at the end of every day and talk for an extended time about mostly non-work-related topics. Initially it was helpful in that these discussions strengthened our relationship, and I knew my boss's heart was in the right place. However, after a month or so, I started to resent these conversations. I wanted to get home at a reasonable hour to be with my family.

It's important to know that I love a quick banter with colleagues around the "water cooler" on any number of topics—family, hobbies, sports, news. The key word here is "quick." The challenge that I faced with my boss is that these conversations were anything but quick. They would extend for lengthy periods—fifteen, twenty, thirty minutes or more.

I dropped subtle hints. I'd start cleaning up the desk area or tactfully mention a family event that we had planned for that evening. Nothing worked. In retrospect, it's obvious that I should have simply approached my boss in a respectful and calm manner. I did consider this. However, he was my boss and had a big influence on my professional future. I wasn't sure how such a conversation would go. It was risky. Ultimately, I weighed my options and, as painful as it was, decided to ride it out.

Here's the vitally important lesson that I learned from this experience: No one is going to tell the boss to stop talking. It's easy to end a conversation with a colleague with a quick "Great talking to you, but I've got to go. Let's catch up later!" Not so with a boss. As was discussed briefly in chapter 4, employees will appear riveted as the boss provides a detailed play-by-play description of their twelve-year-old daughter's latest soccer game. While they appear captivated, the unlucky employee is desperately scrambling for some way—any way—to escape *without* harming the relationship. Not a fun position to be in.

There's an acronym that fits this theme perfectly. It's WAIT, which stand for "Why Am I Talking." It's an excellent reminder that bantering with direct reports is a double-edged sword. Therefore, it is incumbent on you, as the leader, to keep conversations appropriately short. Be respectful of others' time. By demonstrating this subtle sign of respect, you'll better use these interactions as opportunities to build trust.

Another form of disrespect is micromanaging—when the boss provides excessive oversight. Luckily, during my Navy career, I did not work for many micromanaging bosses. Most were great mentors. However, later in my Navy career, I did work for a classic micromanager. What I learned from that experience is that being micromanaged is a form of disrespect. Why? Because the micromanager doesn't respect your skill or talent and will closely observe and control your work, and you won't have much freedom in the workplace. The following story encapsulates well the culture that is created when led by such a boss.

The new boss arrived about two weeks before the Labor Day weekend. As the end of summer approached, the command was finalizing plans to grant an additional vacation day for the majority of our active duty military members. While Monday was a federal holiday for all, active duty members were also given Friday off.[17]

A few days before the holiday weekend, I was informed that the boss wanted a list of all civilian employees who would be working the Friday before the three-day weekend. While some civilian employees elected to take a vacation day, others elected to work on that day. The boss wanted a list of those who elected to work.

I immediately assumed that the boss wanted the list to thank the civilian employees for working on that day. While only a few essential areas of the hospital would remain open (e.g., the emergency room), their presence was critical to keeping these areas up and running. Recognition from the boss would be very well received. I envisioned the boss thanking them via email, or maybe even by writing personal notes, something along the lines of "Thank you! Because of your sacrifice and

---

Leadership Lesson

- Be respectful of others' time.
- Remember that no one is going to tell the boss to stop talking.
- Before you speak, remember to WAIT: *Why Am I Talking.*

dedication to duty, the majority of the active duty staff were able to have a well-deserved additional day off . . . etc., etc."

I knew this would boost morale, and I was excited about the idea. I jumped out of my seat and told my assistant, "This is great! Thanking the civilian staff is perfect. What an awesome opportunity for the boss to show appreciation. Let's get the list together."

My assistant stood in silence. She clearly did not share my enthusiasm.

Shifting nervously, she quietly said, "Ah, sir . . . the boss isn't getting the list together to thank them. The boss will be giving the list to the officer of the day (OOD).[18] The boss has specifically instructed the OOD to periodically check in on each and every civilian employee throughout the day to ensure that they are physically at their place of work . . . and working."

I was stunned. I asked if word of this had gotten out. Word always spreads quickly in military units, and unfortunately this was no exception. The staff knew. The damage was done. That singular act of disrespect derailed the team. Any trust that had been garnered between the boss and civilian staff eroded significantly. The message they received was clear and irrefutable: the boss did not trust them.

How did this erosion in trust impact performance? For the ensuing months until my departure, the civilian staff were uninspired and disengaged. Because they were professionals, they performed their respective jobs, but creativity and innovation were lost. I witnessed a dispirited group that simply came to work and did their jobs. As a small example, their attendance and participation in after-hours command-sponsored events decreased. They were a very experienced, proud, and talented group of professionals, and we'll never know what initiatives and ideas were left on the table.

What's the difference between a great mentor and a micromanager? In a word—respect. Anyone assigned to a new task will require some level of direction and oversight by their boss. When done respectfully, this is called mentoring. When done disrespectfully, it's called micromanaging. Be a great mentor and provide constructive feedback in a respectful manner. Remember that getting to know your staff helps build a foundation of trust; this rule also holds true when mentoring. Tell them about yourself, but spend the majority of time on them. Check in on them and ask how they're doing, especially regarding training. Show the mentee what it takes to be productive and successful. Be enthusiastic and have a positive attitude. Identify the mentee's strengths and weaknesses and respectfully point them out. Be a discerning mentor and be respectful in all your interactions. Remember that the most important aspect of respect is listening. Actually, one of the most important aspects of *leading* is listening. Why is this the case? To answer that question, let's look at the destructive nature of a leader who does *not* listen.

While we all want to be led by competent and confident leaders, no one want to be led by a competent and *arrogant* leader. What makes a leader slip from confidence to arrogance? Arrogant leaders do not listen well. In fact, sometimes they don't listen at all.

While humble leaders listen very well and are eager to learn, arrogant leaders—by their very nature—believe they have all the answers. In meetings, they think they're the smartest ones in the room. Arrogant leaders believe they no longer have a need to learn, grow, or change. Given all this, why *should* they listen?

As an example of their behavior, arrogant leaders often take pride in multitasking. While there is nothing wrong with multitasking, when these leaders are spoken to, they avoid eye contact and continue their

---

Leadership Lesson

A great mentor is a respectful leader who

- provides constructive feedback in a respectful manner
- listens with their heart
- takes time to get to know the mentee and asks how they're doing, especially in regard to their training
- is mindful to not talk too much about themselves
- shows the mentee what it takes to be productive and successful
- is enthusiastic and has a positive attitude
- identifies the mentee's strengths and weaknesses and respectfully points them out
- ensures that the mentee has all resources available for success

work. They clearly have far more important issues to attend to than you. Their actions let you know that they are not interested in you or your concerns.

Arrogant leaders are extremely destructive. Instead of being uplifted and inspired, teams become demoralized, creativity is crushed, and those contributing to the success of the business feel increasingly underappreciated and simply burn out.

Arrogance is one of the most difficult vices for leaders to overcome. How do you prevent it, and what's the antidote? Answer: If you earnestly listen to your people, you will help prevent yourself from slipping into arrogance.

Reflecting back on my years as a leader, and years of observing and studying other leaders, I've concluded that a leader's ability to influence others is directly proportional to the amount of time they're willing to listen to them—to their concerns, challenges, and opinions. Be respectful—spend time listening to your employees.

The leader's level of respect has a significant impact on team culture. Treat staff with respect, and you'll gain trust, increase employee commitment and engagement, and improve team performance. While my examples in this chapter point out both damaging aspects of disrespect and the empowering nature of a respectful leader, there are limitless ways to respect employees and staff. Respectful and humble leaders will create environments where all members of the team can strive to be their best and reach full potential.

KEY POINTS

1. Leaders need to show respect toward their employees. Respect impacts employee engagement more than any other leadership behavior.
2. Times of chaos, tumult, and uncertainty are tremendous opportunities for a leader to positively impact team culture.
3. When bad news comes:
   - Take a breath, thank the messenger, and ask the messenger to thank whoever told them.

- Under no circumstance should you shoot the messenger.
- Remember: This is your crucible moment. How you choose to behave at this moment greatly impacts team culture.
4. A culture of fear breeds unwise decisions. A precursor to a culture of fear—disrespectful behavior—impedes team performance by hindering one's ability to learn, reason, comprehend, plan, and analyze.
5. Be respectful of others' time.
   - Remember that no one is going to tell the boss to stop talking.
   - Before you speak, remember to WAIT: *Why Am I Talking.*
6. A great mentor is a respectful leader who
   - provides constructive feedback in a respectful manner
   - listens with their heart
   - takes time to get to know the mentee and asks how they're doing, especially in regard to their training
   - is mindful to not talk too much about themselves
   - shows the mentee what it takes to be productive and successful
   - is enthusiastic and has a positive attitude
   - identifies the mentee's strengths and weaknesses and respectfully points them out
   - ensures that the mentee has all resources available for success

7

DON'T IGNORE GOOD OR POOR PERFORMANCE

Never miss an opportunity to say a word of congratulation upon anyone's achievement.

—Norman Vincent Peale, *The Power of Positive Thinking*

The highlight of my leadership seminars is interacting with my audience. I especially love to hear of their experiences working for what they describe as "great" leaders. In my seminars, I always try to ask participants to think of great bosses they've worked for, great coaches they've played for, or great teachers they've learned from. I want to know what specific *behaviors* these leaders employed that made them great.

Inevitably a participant will describe such a leader as someone who had recognized them for a specific achievement, milestone, or overall good work. I always ask for details. With swelling enthusiasm and emotion, they'll typically describe the experience in minute detail. It's clear that the experience was profoundly meaningful and impactful. This type of story is *very* common in my seminars.

I then ask them two questions: How long ago did this occur? and How long did the leader speak when they recognized you? Their answers consistently prove the power of not ignoring good performance.

Often these events occurred many years ago—sometimes twenty or twenty-five years! How long did the leader speak? Never more than a few seconds—a minute at best. Despite the passing of time and the fact that these interactions took mere seconds or minutes, the person who received the accolade can vividly recall specific details of the experience as well as the profound impact it had on their morale, motivation, and well-being. Many of these recollections bring forth strong emotions. Sometimes they're accompanied by tears of joy. I'm always amazed at how an extremely short event that occurred years ago can cause such pure, joyful emotion.

While anecdotal stories of employees vividly recalling accolades from years past are thought-provoking, the more practical question to ask is this: Does praise actually improve employee engagement?

Recognition is widely accepted as a vital element in improving motivation.[1] Many studies conducted over the past decades conclude that recognition is a top motivator.[2]

In a more recent study, IBM Smarter Workforce Institute wanted to know the answer to the question posed above: Is there a correlation between employee recognition and employee engagement?[3] IBM researchers surveyed over nineteen thousand workers in twenty-six countries from a variety of industries and jobs. Researchers concluded that there was indeed a strong correlation. Specifically, the study found the following:

- The engagement level of employees who receive recognition is almost three times higher than the engagement level of those who do not.
- Workers who receive recognition are less likely to quit. Without recognition, about half (51 percent) of surveyed employees say they intend to leave, whereas just one-quarter (25 percent) of those who receive recognition say they intend to quit.
- Employees whose organizations use multiple communication channels for recognition are more likely to feel appreciated and show a higher level of employee engagement. The more channels used for recognition, the higher the employee engagement level.
- While not specifically studied, the findings imply that social media platforms could be strong candidates for the effective delivery of recognition, as they offer interactive, frequent, and immediate communication via multiple channels.

Employee recognition is indeed a powerful tool to improve employee engagement. The question then becomes: How best to apply it?

Leadership Lesson

The engagement level of employees who receive recognition is almost three times higher than the engagement level of those who do not.

About a year into my tour as commanding officer, I attended a leadership development seminar in Seattle, Washington. During the seminar, a speaker who was presenting on the importance of accountability mentioned a "praise list." My ears perked up, as I had never heard the term.

As the speaker explained it, a praise list is simply a list of each of your direct reports. Each week, your task as the boss is to find a reason to give each direct report an accolade. After you give the accolade, you place a check mark next to the recipient's name. As the week progresses, you continue to look for reasons to give *each* of your direct reports an accolade. The praise list simply helps ensure that you appropriately recognize *all* your direct reports at least once a week.

During the question-and-answer period of the seminar, an attendee half-jokingly asked a question that I suspect many of the attendees were mulling over. I certainly was.

He smiled and said, "Okay, got it. But what if you can't find a reason during the week to give one of your people an accolade?"

The speaker was no doubt waiting for the question. He smiled back and, after the audience's laughter subsided, said, "Great question! In all seriousness, the answer is either (1) you're not trying hard enough or (2) the person's in the wrong job."

Pretty simple. It's also hard to argue the logic. If you can't find *one thing* during an *entire* workweek for which to recognize one of your employees, either *you* aren't fully engaged or *they* aren't.

That evening, I thought about the dynamics of my board of directors team. This twelve-member team was vitally important to the success of the command. In essence, they ran the day-to-day operations of the hospital. Each member was extremely talented, and during my first year in command, we enjoyed some success. However, I knew we hadn't reached our potential.

I then realized that, like all teams, the board members' individual levels of performance fell into the standard bell curve. While each board member was extremely talented and an invaluable asset to the command, they fell into three general categories: high performers, average performers, and low performers. This was usually dictated by the level of experience they had as board members. We must not misinterpret the terms *average* and *low* here—the average and low performers were extremely talented. Otherwise, they would not have been selected to be board members. Their performance was in relation to the three or four extremely high-functioning and more experienced board members.

That's when I had my revelation. I recalled how I gave ample, and certainly appropriate, praise to the top and average performers. However, I couldn't recall when I had given an accolade to one of the low performers. I asked myself, "Was *I* not engaged or were *they* not engaged?"

It didn't take me long to realize that they were not the ones who were disengaged; it was *me*. I vowed to course correct and use my praise list. Indeed, I found ample oppportunities to recognize them.

In a few weeks the dynamics of the team changed dramatically. Born of a newfound confidence, the "low performers" more freely offered their opinions—many vitally important—on significant issues. The performance of the board improved significantly. We were better informed on issues and, consequently, able to make better decisions.

The key to successfully leveraging a praise list is to proactively find reasons to give accolades. I was very fortunate to have one key member of my leadership team help me appropriately recognize other members of the command outside of the board of directors. While we didn't use a praise list, we achieved success by simply being proactive.

Master Chief Frank Dominguez was one of my command master chiefs during my tenure as commanding officer. On the first Monday morning in his new job, he quietly slipped a piece of paper into my hand. It had the names of four sailors along with brief descriptions of volunteer events these young men and women had supported during the previous weekend—performing humble, unselfish acts of kindness helping organizations like the Special Olympics and serving at a soup kitchen, among others.

He told me that he knew that I liked to walk around the command and thought that it would be good if I recognized these members during my walks. I thanked him profusely. I immediately understood the power of that small piece of paper.

Throughout the ensuing week, during my walks I made a point to visit the areas where these men and women worked. I thanked them for taking time during their day off to volunteer. They were great ambassadors for the Navy and Naval Hospital Bremerton, and I made sure they knew it. It was always a pure joy to see the pride and delight on their faces as I thanked them for these acts of kindness. Many times, they'd look at me in total surprise and ask, "How the heck did you know about this, sir?" I'd tell them that the command master chief was working his magic again. I'd banter a little with everyone but would quickly move on. The entire interaction rarely lasted more than a couple of minutes.

What was the result of these short interactions? To the men and women being recognized, a great deal of pride and satisfaction, as well as a much stronger and trusting relationship between themselves and Master Chief Dominguez. From their perspective, the master chief took the initiative to ensure the commanding officer was aware of their volunteer work, and the commanding officer took the time to thank him. That's a pretty good return on an investment of a couple of minutes.

Further, coworkers who witnessed the interaction no doubt thought a bit more seriously about getting involved in volunteer work. In addition to the satisfaction of volunteering, they may have thought that they'd like similar recognition from the commanding officer. Indeed, the number of staff volunteer hours increased significantly after we started this informal recognition process.

Recognizing an employee for a job well done improves team morale. It's common sense. Why, then, do we elect *not* to go out of our way to recognize our employees?

Here's one reason: We don't fully appreciate the enormous impact a well-timed accolade has and, because of this, we elect not to dedicate the very small amount of time it takes. We're busy. Our to-do list grows. We have unread emails to read, meetings to attend, and phone calls to make. Taking the time to thank someone for a job well done gets relegated to the bottom of the to-do list.

Recall the impressive results of the IBM study: "Engagement levels of employees who receive recognition is almost three times higher than the engagement level of those who do not."

Remember that recognizing employees for good work, and proactively finding the good work, are extremely powerful behaviors that deliver a disproportionate return on investment. A great deal of trust is generated from an interaction that takes mere seconds. Overlooking this practice results in missed opportunities to foster and encourage motivation, creativity, and innovation. Be proactive. Find reasons to recognize your employees. They'll be more engaged, more productive, and more trustful of you as a leader.

Unfortunately, as leaders, we'll also need to address a more challenging issue: the poor performer. This can prove to be quite stressful for any leader. Not surprisingly, most surveys conclude that the number-one stressor for leaders is having to discipline and, if necessary, terminate employees. Why? People generally don't like confrontation. They don't like giving bad news. Having a difficult conversation about an employee's poor performance is challenging. This is tough stuff, and tough stuff just gets tougher the longer you delay addressing it.

One can understand why ignoring poor performance is a behavior that a leader can easily fall prey to. I did just that during the first fifteen years or so of my Navy career. When one of my employees' performance started to slip, I'd tend to ignore it. I'd convince myself that I was being hasty and the performance would improve with time. Unfortunately, it rarely did, and it usually worsened. By the time I did address it, out of frustration, I'd usually overreact.

Leadership Lesson

Each week, find a reason to give each of your direct reports an accolade.

In addition to your standard employee reward and recognition system, proactively find employees who have done good work and thank them face to face during your informal visits (i.e., while walking around).

Like all leaders, I always had a number of pressing issues that needed addressing. Frankly, the vast majority of these tasks were exponentially more enjoyable and rewarding than addressing someone's poor performance. Consequently, taking valuable time for a difficult conversation with an employee would get delayed and continuously relegated to a lower priority in favor of a more "pressing" issue.

What I failed to understand was that addressing poor performance is extremely important. I simply did not appreciate the enormity of what was at stake. Choosing to ignore and not actively address poor performance has dire consequences.

Your employees are always watching you. They're constantly forming and reforming their opinions of you as a leader. They're observing very closely how you handle these difficult workplace situations. Everyone is aware of the level of effort each person on the team is exerting. There are no secrets in this area. When the leader ignores poor performance, often the good performers wonder if you recognize *their* level of effort. When the boss ignores poor performance, employees will form negative opinions about their ability to lead. They'll say that the boss doesn't care, and they'll share these opinions with their coworkers. They'll lose respect, confidence, and trust in the boss.

Fortunately, as a novice leader, I had a modicum of wisdom to know that poor performance would eventually need to be addressed. I was cognizant that if I continued to ignore the poor performance, other members of my team would certainly take note, and not in a good way—it would send the message that a lower level of performance was acceptable. How could one conclude otherwise? By definition, the fact that I didn't address it indeed made such a lower level of effort acceptable. The performance level is not created by what you say; it's created by what you tolerate. Tolerating poor performance makes it acceptable.

Leadership Lesson

When the boss ignores poor performance, employees will lose respect, confidence, and trust in their leader.

Inevitably, others will cautiously test the waters. Like an infection, the longer we let it fester, the more it spreads, and a growing number would conclude that the lower level of effort is indeed acceptable. Others will justifiably get angry at the blatant unfairness of the whole affair and freely share their anger with colleagues around the water cooler. What's at stake when a leader neglects to address poor performance? Trust in them as a leader, as well as a cumulative lowering of overall team performance and acceptance of a lower standard.

As mentioned, early on in my career I'd ignore poor performance in the hope that it would resolve on its own. When I eventually got around to addressing it, I'd treat the interaction as a simple check in the box. It was only one of many items I needed to take care of that day. I'd schedule maybe fifteen or twenty minutes for the meeting, including a couple of minutes prior to prepare and organize my thoughts. The conversation would focus on how their lower level of effort was impacting the mission. I'd no doubt add how this would set a bad example for others, probably ending with a bit of a pep talk to help motivate the individual to get back on track. I had hundreds of conversations similar to this early on in my career. They covered a vast array of performance issues, and the results varied greatly. The only constant was the fact that I was always glad to have it over with. I'd put a nice neat check in that box and move on to the next issue. I failed to appreciate the enormity of what was at stake as a result of these conversations.

At about the fifteen-year mark of my Navy career, I was put in charge of a hospital pharmacy operation that had significant performance issues. The primary issue was patient complaints—there were lots of them! The top two patient complaints were (1) the wait to get a prescription filled was too long and (2) rude behavior on the part of my staff. Both complaints were legitimate. Changes were needed.

Leadership Lesson

The team's performance level is not created by what you say; it's created by what you tolerate.

My task was to turn the department around. I was extremely busy at home and at work. Kris and I had three young children at home, and time management was a big challenge. To make it all work, I vowed to be more efficient with my time. What did I learn from this experience? You can't be efficient when it comes to personnel issues. More simply, don't be efficient with people.

The solutions to the causes of these complaints were pretty straightforward. Updated robotic technology was the answer to expediting the prescription-filling process. Researching these robots was fun. I diligently scheduled a few thirty-minute blocks of time each week to learn about specifications, purchase prices, lease prices, and other details of different robots. I arranged a series of meetings with my leadership team to discuss and debate the nuances of the different products. We eventually purchased the right robot at a good price. The processing time for filling prescriptions decreased, and patient complaints regarding excessive wait times all but disappeared.

The other issue that needed to be addressed was the rude behavior exhibited by the pharmacy staff. Prior to my arrival, members of the pharmacy team weren't held accountable when they exhibited rude behavior. Bad habits had developed. To resolve this, I communicated my expectation that *all* patients were to *always* be treated with respect, modeled that behavior, and held staff accountable when they didn't meet those expectations. Pretty standard stuff. However, these bad habits had evolved over a period of years. Again, the staff had not been held accountable. To course correct, I knew there were a number of one-on-one meetings in my future.

Was I flexible regarding how long these one-on-one meetings lasted? Unfortunately, I was not. Time management was my mantra, and each meeting was rigidly scheduled for a maximum of thirty minutes. Some meetings ended in a matter of minutes. Others consumed the full half hour. Regardless of the tack these meetings took, I never exceeded my thirty-minute time cap. I had a schedule to keep. I needed to be efficient. It turns out that I couldn't have been more wrong.

While we eventually decreased the number of patient complaints regarding rude behavior, the process was agonizingly slow. I've thought long and hard about that experience. What did I learn? In my zeal to be efficient with my time, I scheduled my one-on-one meetings to course correct rude behavior with the same inflexibility as when I scheduled meetings to discuss buying new robots. That was a mistake. Not surprisingly, the vast majority of the one-on-one meetings with staff members to correct rude behavior were exceedingly more difficult to manage. Many of these meetings evoked emotional reactions. That's not surprising. People have needs and concerns. They harbor a range of emotions— fear, anger, stress, hostility, sadness, and guilt, among a host of others. Robots, data, specifications, purchase prices, and lease prices, however, don't.

Meetings to discuss a behavioral change can trigger unpredictable emotions. Allow for this unpredictability. You may be near a breakthrough. Allow time to reach that important breakthrough. Here's a practical tip: When scheduling these meetings, ensure flexibility in your schedule. In other words, ensure that your schedule allows this meeting to continue, if necessary, past the scheduled time.

Later in my career, when I appreciated the importance of these meetings, I ensured that my schedule was flexible. Many difficult conversations I had with staff members would continue well past their scheduled time. Often, the staff member would recognize that we were beyond the scheduled time and voice their concern. I'd respectfully say that if their schedule permitted (not surprisingly, it always did!), I'd like to continue, always adding that I considered this a very important conversation (because it was). That is a very strong message: the boss is willing to invest as much time as needed to resolve the issue. What did I learn? I learned that this was no time to be efficient. I learned that it was OK to sacrifice expediency in order to be effective. When dealing with course correcting an employee, it was a valuable lesson.

I learned another important lesson from this experience. While I diligently invested hours preparing for my meetings to discuss which robot to buy (debating specifications, prices, and other aspects of different vendors), I did *not* invest appropriate time preparing for my one-on-one meetings to course correct an employee's rude behavior. Before a difficult conversation, it's extremely important to prepare. Remind yourself of the importance of staying calm. Choose your words wisely. Be mindful of your body language (i.e., don't cross your arms, and be conscious of your facial expressions). Don't have any physical barriers between you and your employee. Lastly, practice with a trusted colleague; they'll be able to give you valuable feedback about your body language and your choice of words.

I was several years into my career before I grasped the significance of devoting effort, thought, and time to changing poor performance. However, I finally came to appreciate that these conversations directly dictated the performance and productivity of an important human capital investment—the Navy had invested thousands of dollars in the person whose behavior I was trying to change—both in the short term and in the long term. These conversations would result in their performance either improving or getting worse. More importantly, their trust in me as a leader would change accordingly. In *every* case, the status quo changed. More times than not, it changed significantly.

As mentioned earlier, while we eventually decreased the number of complaints regarding rudeness, the process was agonizingly slow. I now understand that if I had invested time preparing for these conversations as well as allowed more flexibility in my schedule to extend these conversations, we would have found success much faster.

During my command tour, when I had a much clearer understanding of the enormity of what was at stake with these conversations, I had an exceptionally lengthy and difficult conversation with one of my officers regarding his annual evaluation. In this case, he was not a classic poor performer. The problem was that he was surrounded by officers who had performed better, a challenging situation that is not uncommon in any organization. In any case, this officer was very upset that he did not get a better evaluation and wanted to know why. The bottom line is that it was a very difficult conversation.

It's important to note that in the U.S. military, an officer's annual evaluation is *the* primary factor in determining which officers are pro-

---

Leadership Lesson

When dealing with employee performance issues, it's OK to sacrifice expediency in order to be more effective. Be flexible with your time.

moted to the next rank and which are not. Each officer within a command is essentially ranked against their peers. An officer's future in the military is dictated by this ranking. At a certain point in an officer's career, it's up or out. Either you get promoted or you're a civilian. To reach retirement eligibility, an officer must have a minimum of twenty years of service. This is a fair but extremely competitive process. In this particular officer's case, because of this evaluation, he was justifiably concerned about his ability to get to his twenty-year mark.

The conversation happened to be scheduled on the Friday after Thanksgiving. The hospital was quiet, as most staff were home enjoying time with their families. I was hoping to do the same. My plan for that day was a couple hours of cleaning up some emails and signing some routine correspondence, and then home by noon. When I saw on my schedule that I was to meet with this officer in the early afternoon, I knew my day would not be short.

Immediately after seeing the meeting on my schedule, I started to prepare. I reread his evaluation, his peers' evaluations, and other pertinent information. I talked to my executive officer (XO), Commander Kurt Houser, and Command Master Chief Tom Countryman—both extraordinarily talented leaders—to get their advice regarding this officer's performance. (As a side note, as part of my decision-making process on any important issue, I'd solicit input from my senior NCOs [members of the chief's mess]—they always gave me wise counsel.) I wrote this all down and practiced what I wanted to say. While I didn't know how the meeting would proceed or how it would end, I did know one thing—there was much at stake. His trust in me as a leader was going to change. It was going to either increase or decrease—it would not stay the same. Either he'd walk away upset, stay upset, and quite possibly turn into a festering problem or he'd walk away appropriately disappointed but remain a hard-working, engaged, productive member of the command. Those were the stark choices. Amazingly, the only factors that would dictate the outcome were the words that came out of my mouth and, to a certain degree, my body language.

I don't recall exactly how long we spoke. Maybe two hours. However, I vividly recall how difficult it was. I explained to him as honestly as I could the reason for his evaluation. Throughout the discussion, I kept reminding myself what was at stake. I also reminded myself to stay calm and to focus on listening. I tried to discipline myself to not form my thoughts as he spoke. At one point, he expressed concern that the meeting was going well past its scheduled time (one hour). As mentioned earlier, continuing the conversation past the scheduled time sends a strong message that the boss is willing to invest as much time as needed to reach an understanding. When one appreciates what's at stake, it's the right investment to make. At the end of the conversation, I knew we had reached a partial breakthrough. While disappointed, he better understood the reasons for his evaluation and what he needed to do to compete with his peers going forward.

Over the ensuing year he stayed engaged, continued to work hard, and earned a more competitive evaluation. I followed this officer's career from afar and saw that he continued to grow as a leader; he was promoted to the next rank at regular intervals and overall did great work for the Navy.

Was the extra hour we spent together worth it? Was the time I used to prepare for the meeting worth it? Did my command, and the Navy, get an adequate return on these small investments in time? I think the answers to all these questions is "yes."

Let's talk about another simple but powerful technique that a leader can use to more effectively address a poor performer. The key is getting to the root cause of the issue. To unleash this powerful tool, the leader is simply seeking to understand why the performance is diminishing. Let me tell you a story that will help explain how this technique is an absolute game changer when dealing with a performance issue.

I had just arrived as XO of U.S. Naval Hospital Rota, Spain. My unpacked boxes of books and professional papers were still piled high against the wall in my office when I was informed that one of the officers who worked for me, Commander King, had completely lost his cool and berated a secretary the previous afternoon. Commander King had just returned from a business trip in the United States and was upset because something had gone wrong with his rental car reservation. He confronted the secretary and lit into her. Reportedly his outburst had her in tears.

Fresh from Command Leadership School in Newport, Rhode Island, I looked at this as a great opportunity. Addressing this outburst of anger would give me the opportunity to get an important message out

---

Leadership Lesson: Tips for Having a Difficult Conversation

- If your gut is telling you that the status quo is not acceptable, you must act.
- Seek wise counsel from a trusted colleague or mentor. Discuss the situation, and ask for guidance.
- Remind yourself of what's at stake: the employee's future contribution to the organization, as well as your employee's confidence and trust in you as a leader.
- Invest appropriate time preparing for the meeting.
- Practice with a trusted colleague.
- Choose your words wisely, and be aware of the inflection of your voice and the volume of your words, facial expressions, and general body language.
- Listen with your heart. Absorb what you're hearing.
- Don't have any physical barriers—for example, a desk—between you and your employee.
- Stay calm.

---

to everyone: treating people with respect was a top priority. My expectation was that people who worked for me were to *always* treat *all* staff with dignity and respect. Given that I had just gotten to the command, I could quickly set the tone that berating fellow employees was not tolerated.

Commander King reported to my office later that day. After exchanging some pleasantries, I told him I could understand his frustration over the rental car fiasco, as it had happened to me during my career. I told him that we'd look into what happened and try to fix it so it wouldn't happen again. If, by chance, it did recur, he should let his chain of command, including me, know. Changing tack, I told him in the future he should refrain from taking his frustration out on another shipmate. In closing, I stated my expectation that we are to treat each other with respect.

The good news is that over the ensuing two years, I never heard of any similar incidences from Commander King. Nor did I get any similar reports from other officers. Thinking about the incident at the end of that two-year assignment, it appeared that my early intervention with Commander King had an impact on rude behavior. That was good news. However, over that two-year tour of duty, Commander King and I maintained a professional, but distant, relationship. He was an extraordinarily talented officer and did his job very well. Despite his abundant talent, he didn't contribute to the command as much as he could have. At the end of his tour in Rota, he decided to terminate his commission in the Navy and pursue private practice. This was a loss to the Navy, as we needed all hands on deck, especially from talented officers like him, to fight the wars then being waged in Iraq and Afghanistan.

Fast-forward a few years, and I'm in command at Naval Hospital Bremerton. From my first day in command, I communicated that one of my primary expectations was for *all* staff to *always* treat *everyone* with dignity and respect. One evening, about two years into that tour, my XO came into my office to discuss the day's events. This was routine business and a relaxing way to end the day. At the end of the conversation, he mentioned that there was one additional odd event he wanted to tell me about. He mentioned that it appeared that one of our officers had berated one of our secretaries over the phone.

I immediately thought of the incident in Rota and said to myself, "Here we go again . . ."

He explained that the officer, Commander Allen, had lost his temper because a secretary moved his very expensive bicycle without his permission. I asked him, "What did Commander Allen say, exactly?"

"Oh, sir, he left a voice message for the secretary. The secretary sent it to me. I've got the message, sir. Do you want to hear it?"

"By all means, let's hear it," I responded.

We moved to the XO's office and heard the message. Commander Allen's loud and angry voice filled the room. He had clearly lost his temper. The tirade was filled with ample colorful language. It was bad.

Listening intently, I could feel my anger rising. I'm sure my ears grew red with fury as the ugly barrage of words continued. It was very hard to contain my rage and bitter disappointment. I'd been in command two years, and Commander Allen knew me well. Specifically, he knew my expectations regarding civility.

Seeing my mounting anger, the XO immediately shot up out of his chair and fervently blurted out, "Sir, let's bring him up here right now! Sir, you've been talking about treating people with respect since you've been here. This is inexcusable, sir!"

It was obvious that the XO wanted to see the public hanging right then and there.

I let his comments linger for a couple of seconds. That was *very* tempting. However, something told me to slow down. Something told me that I needed to "seek to understand." I calmly told the XO that I wanted to sleep on it and that we'd discuss it the next day. What gave me such wisdom?

Some things you can't make up, and this story falls into that category. On the very morning of this incident with Commander Allen, I followed my morning routine of dropping the kids off at their schools and listening to one of many leadership/self-help CDs I habitually played on my twenty-minute commute to the hospital. The CD that I arbitrarily grabbed that morning was Stephen Covey's timeless book *The 7 Habits of Highly Effective People*. The morsel of wisdom Dr. Covey gave to me that morning was one of his habits.

Dr. Covey told me, "Seek first to understand, then be understood—use empathetic listening to genuinely understand a person, which compels them to reciprocate the listening and take an open mind to being influenced by you."[4]

It was by sheer luck that I heard these wise words only a few hours before hearing Commander Allen's telephone tirade. It was a bizarre coincidence. Reflecting back on Commander Allen's past performance, he had never acted in this manner before. He was very well liked and enjoyed a great reputation as a hard worker and well-respected officer. As mentioned, it was also true that Commander Allen was well aware of my expectation regarding civil behavior. This episode—losing his temper with a secretary over something as silly as moving a bike—clearly did not make sense. I was eager to talk with Commander Allen the following day.

The next morning, Commander Allen sheepishly entered my office. I told him that I wanted to talk to him about the angry phone message he left for his secretary. Using Dr. Covey's sage advice, I calmly said, "Help me understand why this incident occurred."

Knowing that this would most likely be a difficult conversation, I ensured flexibility in my schedule—my next scheduled meeting was not urgent. That was very fortunate because our conversation went well past the scheduled time. He was, first and foremost, embarrassed about the incident. He apologized for his actions and agreed to apologize to the secretary. More importantly, he opened up to me regarding issues taking place in his personal life. He told me a gut-wrenching story of a man whose personal life was being tested to the extreme. A close family member was fighting a severe illness, among other significant issues. Needless to say, the meeting was emotional. Other than showing compassion and encouraging him to seek professional counseling, which he agreed to, there was nothing else to do. After regaining his composure, Commander Allen stood up, walked to the door, and, before leaving, turned to me. He locked eyes on me and said with full conviction, "Sir, thank you. If there is *anything* you need from me, please let me know. Thank you again, sir."

I made it a point to visit Commander Allen every couple of weeks to make sure his life was getting back on track. Indeed, he was on the mend. It was clear that he was grateful to have been given the opportunity to tell me of the extreme stresses in his life. This certainly helped explain his aberrant behavior. On a somewhat different note, I was equally grateful that Dr. Covey gave me such wise counsel hours before this incident. Given my initial anger when I first heard Commander Allen's unruly phone message, I'm not sure how I would have reacted without this advice. (As a side note, this is an excellent example of the need to continuously learn the art of leadership, which will be discussed in chapter 9.)

A few weeks after this incident, I had my scheduled one-on-one meeting with my boss. She noted a deficiency in one of our key performance indicators—our periodic colonoscopy screenings.[5] Naval Hospital Bremerton was responsible for the health care of approximately forty-five thousand patients, some of whom required periodic colonoscopy screenings. We had not performed the procedure on some patients who required it, and that needed to be fixed. The challenge with colonoscopy screenings is that many departments have critical functions to ensure success, but no *one* department is responsible. We needed to assign a person to coordinate the efforts across these different departments. We needed a champion, and I needed to decide who that champion would be.

The first person I thought of was Commander Allen. He was an excellent choice to get the colonoscopy screenings in order. I knocked on his office door and awaited a response.

"Come in," I heard him say from his office.

As I entered his office, Commander Allen jumped up from his chair and excitedly said, "Sir, great to see you again! What brings you up here?" I told him of the challenge we were facing with the colonoscopy screenings. I then said, "I'm looking for a champion. I need someone to lead the effort and . . ." Before I could finish my sentence, he pleaded, "Please, sir, let me take it." Without a moment of hesitation, I told him the project was his.

To this day, I'm really not sure how we performed so many colon-oscopies in such a short time. Regardless, we were able to schedule and complete all backlogged colonoscopies within a matter of a few weeks. When my boss noted the rapid turnaround, she asked jokingly if we were doing "drive-by" colonoscopies. I told her that Commander Allen's leadership was the reason for the remarkable performance. It was true. He did an absolutely phenomenal job.

Let's compare the conversations I had with Commander King and Commander Allen and their aftermath. Both officers needed course correction after their angry outbursts. My expectation was that members of my team would treat everyone with respect. They both knew it and both failed to meet that expectation.

In Commander King's case, I respectfully, but directly, told him to not repeat the mistake. I made no attempt to "seek first to understand." What was the outcome? We had no similar incidences from Commander King or any other command members during the ensuing two years. That's the good news. The bad news is that while Commander King quietly did his job, despite being extremely talented, he didn't contribute to the command nearly as much as he could have. Further, he decided to terminate his commission in the Navy and pursue private practice after that tour.

With Commander Allen, however, the first words out of my mouth when we met were "help me understand why this incident occurred."

Again, I was lucky to have been given such wise counsel so soon before the incident. Because of that sage advice, I showed empathy. I earnestly wanted to understand. How did that turn out? We had a passionately devoted employee who, when given the opportunity to prove his worth, performed miraculously. How many colon cancers did we diagnose during that blitz of colonoscopies? How many lives did we save? We'll never know, but no doubt a number of cancers were detected early. This can all be attributed to Commander Allen's zeal to perform.

All leaders will encounter a person whose poor performance needs addressing. Having a difficult conversation regarding an employee's poor performance is challenging. However, by "seeking first to understand," you're earnestly trying to understand why the performance is subpar. You're showing open-mindedness, empathy, and patience. In order to seek to understand, you cannot judge—you must admit that you don't currently understand and you're trying to see things from the other person's point of view.

Why do we tend not to do this? Why do we speak first? In most cases, it's because we're looking for people to understand *us*. However, when we speak first, we may well say something that we'll regret. Like toothpaste squeezed out of a tube, once it's out, you can't get it back in. If we seek to understand first, we're more likely to listen and, therefore, be better informed. When we *do* speak, we'll speak with more wisdom.

In the end, you're proving that you *care* about understanding the other person's point of view. You're projecting the idea that you value that individual. Leaders who seek first to understand by listening without trying to formulate a solution or response at the same time—just *listen*—convey support, collaboration, openness, and sincere caring. Seeking first to understand generates *enormous* trust.

The next time you need to have a difficult conversation with an employee who is not meeting your expectations, think of this story. You have a choice regarding how you'll interact. Your interaction can be similar to the one I had with Commander King, or it can look like the one I had with Commander Allen. Both can change behavior, as was the case with these officers. However, when you seek first to understand, as I did with Commander Allen, it's an act of caring that can create enormous trust.

How often can a leader resort to using the "seek first to understand"

Leadership Lesson

When addressing an employee who is not meeting your expectations, start the conversation by asking, "Help me understand why . . ." Then listen with your heart.

---

behavior with the same poor performer? Not often. The leader's responsibility is to identify what needs to be changed, understand why it's happening, and help motivate the employee to initiate the change. However, at the end of the day, it's the responsibility of the employee to change. It is *their* responsibility, not *yours*. If having the "seek first to understand" discussion does not result in the employee changing their behavior, you'll need to continue the dialogue with other leadership tools. Poor performance needs to be addressed, albeit with other tactics, until the problem is resolved. I was faced with this situation more than once in my career. Let me share one story that occurred during my chief of staff, Navy Medicine West tour.

Very early in that tour, it was brought to my attention that Dan, a civilian employee and an important member of the Navy Medicine West team, was frequently rude to other team members. Dan had numerous complaints lodged against him. Dan's position required him to devote about 75 percent of his time to technical work and 25 percent of his time to interacting with other team members. He was excellent with the former, terrible with the latter.

Not surprisingly, members of the team avoided him. They simply didn't want to deal with his abrasiveness. This situation was impacting our team performance and, if left unchecked, would soon impact mission accomplishment. It was clear that I needed to talk with Dan.

We met in my office and, after exchanging some pleasantries, spent some time getting to know one another (Dan was not my direct report, and this was our first meeting). I complimented him on his mastery of the technical part of his job. I then calmly mentioned the inordinate number of complaints lodged against him. I said calmly, "Help me understand what's going on."

Dan didn't get upset or angry. He explained that he had some personal issues that he was sorting out. He was under a lot of pressure, and that was causing his poor behavior. I was sympathetic and encouraged him to seek professional help, which we both agreed was readily available. At the end of our meeting, I again complimented him on his technical mastery and reminded him how his rude behavior was impacting team performance. I encouraged him to get professional help and made it very clear that his behavior needed to change. We agreed to meet again.

Unfortunately, over the ensuing weeks, I continued to get reports that Dan's abrasive behavior had not changed. It was time to move on from "seek first to understand" to other techniques. We met twice more within a couple of weeks and talked about the continued complaints. Despite having ample opportunities to get professional help, he did not. He didn't explain why but ardently stated that he was trying to change his behavior. I explained that he gave me no choice but to begin the process of terminating his employment.

Dan quit about a week after our last meeting. I was informed that he was hired into a new position that required lots of technical expertise and little interaction with coworkers—a much better fit for him. When I informed my boss, Admiral Forrest Faison, of this latest development, he said, "Remember, Mark, everyone has a seat on the bus. Sometimes they're on the wrong bus. You got Dan on the right bus!"

How true! I love the logic of those words and repeat them often. People sometimes don't perform well because the job is simply not a good match for their strength, skill, talent, or passion. In any case, the leader has three choices with poor performers—train, transfer, or terminate.

Regarding training, make sure you work with the employee to establish realistic goals. Make sure they have the training to achieve these goals and that they're aware of their areas for improvement. Create an action plan for improvement. If the job doesn't match the employee's strengths, find one that does. If none of these alternatives work, terminating the employee may be the right decision.

In regard to addressing a poor performer, the leader's overall goal is to retain the employee, meet operational needs, and provide meaningful and rewarding work to everyone involved. The employee was hired because there was promise in their skills, motivations, and capability. The leader's job is to search for the root cause of the poor performance, whether it can be found within your department or elsewhere, and find a solution. When done with openness, honesty, and empathy, it shows that you care. This creates trust because people feel supported to reach their performance potential. They feel valued, knowing that the organization wants to find a good fit for their abilities.

Difficult conversations regarding performance are absolutely golden opportunities to earn trust. Take the time to gather your thoughts and practice for these difficult conversations. Treat them with the same respect you would a capital investment decision. Allow for the unpre-

---

Leadership Lesson

Every employee has a seat on the bus. Some are on the wrong bus. A leader's job is to get them on the right bus. The employee may not be properly trained for the job, or the job might not be a good match for their strength, skill, talent, or passion. In any case, the leader has three choices: train, transfer, or terminate.

- Train: Did you as the leader "seek first to understand" to find the root cause of the poor performance? Did you and the employee work collaboratively to establish realistic goals? Does the employee have adequate training to achieve these goals? Have you shown them their areas of improvement? Have you developed an action plan for improvement and a path to success?
- Transfer: Does the job match the employee's strengths? Is it a good fit? If not, are there alternative roles that would be a better fit for their strengths?
- Terminate: We certainly don't want to instantly revert to finding "new buses" for poor performers. However, we need to be mindful that if performance does not improve despite employing the aforementioned techniques, terminating the employee may be the right decision.

dictability that comes with human emotion; don't be efficient with people. In other words, it's OK to sacrifice expediency in order to be more effective. Ensure that your meeting after a difficult one-on-one conversation can be delayed or canceled with little difficulty or consequence.

Before we leave this chapter, it's important to remember that trust in a leader is tenuous. It's fickle. As a leader, you can diligently employ all other behaviors described so far in this book—know your staff, be visible, and treat them with respect—but if you don't address poor performance, respect in you as a leader will erode significantly.

KEY POINTS

1. The engagement level of employees who receive recognition is almost three times higher than the engagement level of those who do not.
2. Each week, find a reason to give each of your direct reports an accolade. Proactively find employees who have done good work and thank them face to face during your informal visits (i.e., while walking around).
3. When the boss ignores poor performance, employees will lose respect, confidence, and trust in their leader.
4. The team's performance level is not created by what you say; it's created by what you tolerate.
5. When dealing with employee performance issues, it's OK to sacrifice expediency in order to be more effective. Be flexible with your time.
6. Tips for having a difficult conversation:
   - If your gut is telling you that the status quo is not acceptable, you must act.
   - Seek wise counsel from a trusted colleague or mentor. Discuss the situation, and ask for guidance.
   - Remind yourself of what's at stake: the employee's future contribution to the organization, as well as your employee's confidence and trust in you as a leader.
   - Invest appropriate time preparing for the meeting.
   - Practice with a trusted colleague.

- Choose your words wisely, and be aware of the inflection of your voice and the volume of your words, facial expressions, and general body language.
- Listen with your heart. Absorb what you're hearing.
- Don't have any physical barriers—for example, a desk—between you and your employee.
- Stay calm.

7. When addressing an employee who is not meeting your expectations, start the conversation by asking, "Help me understand why . . ." Then listen with your heart.

8. Every employee has a seat on the bus. Some are on the wrong bus. A leader's job is to get them on the right bus. The employee may not be properly trained for the job, or the job might not be a good match for their strength, skill, talent, or passion. In any case, the leader has three choices: train, transfer, or terminate.

- Train: Did you as the leader "seek first to understand" to find the root cause of the poor performance? Did you and the employee work collaboratively to establish realistic goals? Does the employee have adequate training to achieve these goals? Have you shown them their areas of improvement? Have you developed an action plan for improvement and a path to success?
- Transfer: Does the job match the employee's strengths? Is it a good fit? If not, are there alternative roles that would be a better fit for their strengths?
- Terminate: We certainly don't want to instantly revert to finding "new buses" for poor performers. However, we need to be mindful that if performance does not improve despite employing the aforementioned techniques, terminating the employee may be the right decision.

8

OPTIMISM

A leader is a dealer in hope.

—Napoleon Bonaparte

Bound for Antarctica, Sir Ernest Shackleton boldly planned to be the
first human to cross the last uncharted continent on foot. Born in
Ireland in 1874, he was a polar explorer who had led two previous British
expeditions to the Antarctic and one of the principal figures of the period
known as the "Heroic Age of Antarctic Exploration."

On this third expedition, his ship, the *Endurance*, and twenty-nine
hand-selected men set sail from England in August 1914. In January
1915, after battling its way for six weeks through a thousand miles of the
world's worst weather and now only a day's sail short of her destination,
the *Endurance* became locked inside the deadly pack ice.

Sleeping on the *Endurance* each night, crew members could hear the
strange and frightening sounds of the ship's timbers slowly being crushed
by the massive, shifting ice floe. All knew their fate. The *Endurance*
would succumb to nature's unrelenting power. She would sink. The
crew would be forced to spend the long, cold polar winter trying to
survive on the active ice floe—four months of complete darkness scrap-
ing by on an ever-decreasing supply of food and other critical provisions.

Oddly, despite this extremely perilous situation, morale among the
crew remained high. Reading diary entries from the members of the
crew, it's clear that all shared an attitude of optimism and hopefulness.
To a man, they had little doubt that they would survive. And they were
right. Miraculously, against tremendous odds, *all* crew members lived to
tell of their amazing two-year odyssey of survival.

This story is simply astonishing on many levels. From a leadership perspective, the most astounding element is the optimism clearly shared by all crew members, which is wonderfully depicted in a remarkable photograph taken during the expedition. Despite the undeniable peril the men faced, the photo below shows crew members joyfully playing soccer in the snow and ice with the *Endurance* far in the background, notably locked in the crushing ice floe.

Given the extreme peril the men faced when the photograph was taken, how could they be enjoying a leisurely soccer game?

The answer is Shackleton's tremendous leadership and, specifically during this expedition, his remarkable ability to create a culture of optimism. Morrell and Capparell note, "Shackleton believed in optimism, lived it, selected the crew for it, talked about it, and praised crewmembers when they showed it. Optimism became the culture so that the men continued to keep their spirits up."[1]

As mentioned, against all odds, all twenty-nine men survived the harrowing and miraculous two-year ordeal. No matter how dire the situation, Shackleton *never* deviated from his upbeat, can-do, optimistic demeanor. His infectious optimism, which inspired the trust of his men, was the key component that ensured the team's survival.

Iconic photograph of Ernest Shackleton's crew playing soccer on the ice shelf. When this photo was taken, these men knew that they were facing an epic battle for survival.

A leader's overall optimistic demeanor, when routinely displayed, benefits the workplace environment in several ways. It gives employees hope that great things are possible from their efforts. It helps make their day-to-day work feel richer and more meaningful. An optimistic leader generates confidence in the greater cause, which, in turn, inspires trust in the leader. This makes lofty goals and great feats—like that of Shackleton's men—feel within reach.

After transitioning from the Navy, I worked for a short time in corporate sales. Our boss, Mel, who had vast corporate knowledge and keen business acumen, led our sales team. I learned a great deal about the corporate world from him and remain thankful that he gave me the opportunity. Unfortunately, while Mel understood the technical aspects of business, he also had a major shortcoming: Mel *always* saw the glass as half empty.

During my first week on the job, I came to understand that the entire team was behind on our sales targets, and this topic was appropriately the primary discussion point at our weekly meetings. I remember well my first weekly meeting. There were many unhappy faces around the table. Pessimism permeated the room. "Not a lot of joy among these folks," I remember thinking. The meeting started with an employee proudly and enthusiastically announcing that he had secured a new client.

My immediate thought was "Wow, some good news. The boss can recognize this and get the team a little fired up!" Instead of celebrating, the boss dryly and glumly stated, "We'll need a lot more success—more than this one client—to reach our sales goals." I looked around the table at the other members of the team. What little energy had been in the room—and there wasn't much to begin with—quickly vanished. All heads went down, some shaking back and forth.

Leadership Lesson

A leader's optimism gives others hope that great things are possible from their efforts.

I quickly came to understand that Mel was a pessimist. The meetings that he led were always depressing. No accolades. No victories celebrated. Instead, he would remind us of our poor sales performance during the previous quarters. The negative drumbeat was relentless. The people on that sales team were a dispirited collection of extremely talented men and women led by pessimism, gloom, and cynicism.

After a handful of these meetings, and having been onboard for a couple of months, I mustered the courage to talk to Mel. At our next scheduled one-on-one meeting, after some pleasantries and business discussion, Mel asked me how I was doing. I respectfully asked if I could share some thoughts about what I had observed over the past few weeks. He told me that he'd love my perspective.

I mentioned that while the victories were not as plentiful as any of us would like, we certainly had *some* good news to celebrate. I gave him some examples and gently suggested that he begin and end his meetings by mentioning these small victories. Mel appeared to listen.

Unfortunately, he proceeded to remind me in great detail of the recent missteps we'd encountered during the past quarter. His account of the poor status of our department went on for forty-five minutes. At its conclusion, I was as pessimistic as he was! Further, I was convinced that there was no way he was going to change his behavior. Indeed, Mel never changed, and the team suffered greatly. We continued to flounder and never came close to reaching our potential. Three months after our discussion, there were numerous firings within the sales team. Mel was one of the victims.

From that experience, I learned once again the destructive power of pessimism. Its power lies in its infectiousness. A leader's contagious pessimism will infect those whom they lead. Employees will be less

---

Leadership Lesson

Teams led by pessimistic leaders underperform in the fog of malaise, helplessness, and passivity; they're easily overwhelmed by even a meager challenge.

hopeful, focused, and motivated. The result is a cynical, demoralized, and deflated team that struggles to hit its stride. These teams woefully underperform. In the fog of malaise, helplessness, and passivity, they're easily overwhelmed when faced with even a meager challenge. As this downward spiral escalates, trust in both their leaders and colleagues erodes.

One of the truly remarkable and rewarding tours of duty I had during my Navy career was with a small group of highly motivated doctors and pharmacists from all three services—Army, Navy, and Air Force. These professionals were all hand-picked to join a newly formed team that was directed to reduce the escalating cost of prescription medications provided for all Department of Defense (DoD) active duty Army, Navy, and Air Force members and their families. Our challenging task was to reduce costs without decreasing quality of care. At that time, there were over eight million men, women, and children eligible for prescription medications throughout DoD. The annual cost was over $5 billion and climbing fast.

Our boss, Dom, was a brilliant, hardworking, and extremely passionate leader who was highly respected by all. Dom cared for us, and we cared for him. We were a tight group. We treated each other as family. Dom's passion was contagious, and he quickly established a culture of caring, hard work, and trust. We were poised for success. Because I was senior to other members of the team, Dom selected me to be his deputy.

The idea of creating a small team to bend the cost curve for the entire DoD pharmacy benefit was novel; it had never been tried before. While the team shared a genuine passion for this noble and ambitious undertaking, early on wins were few and far between.

Leadership Lesson

Great leaders know that pessimism is poison. Its lethality lies in its insidious infectiousness.

After the six-month honeymoon period ended, enthusiasm was slowly replaced with frustration. Every morning we'd meet with Dom to share the progress or, more accurately, lack of progress with our respective projects. It was slow and insidious at first, but sarcasm crept into the meetings. A few of the more vocal naysayers would spew their negative comments, and Dom and I would make meager attempts to mitigate the damage or, in times of weakness, simply join in. These meetings frequently went much longer than scheduled, drained everyone of energy, and were generally recognized to be pretty much a waste of time. In short, neither Dom nor I *led* these meetings. We *attended* them. One could feel the energy, passion, and trust dissipate like air leaking from a balloon.

We fell into this easy trap because we didn't recognize the volatility of team culture, and, more importantly, we didn't appreciate the influence we wielded in creating that culture. In fact, these meetings were golden opportunities to positively impact the culture, but we took our eyes off the ball and simply neglected to lead. While we had established a foundation of trust during our first six months, the foundation was being eroded by the growing sense of frustration and pessimism. This was a perfect case study of a well-known leadership maxim: Workplace atmosphere can be hijacked by discouraged employees if not monitored and "massaged" by the leader. This is exactly what happened with our small team of motivated and talented members.

As time progressed, Dom's level of frustration and worry could be easily read on his face. The morning meeting would start with Dom entering the room with a scowl. We'd grind through the meeting and return to our desks drained of any temporary energy the morning cups of coffee mercifully offered.

I've always had great mentors whom I've leaned on when I knew things needed a course correction, and we desperately needed a course correction. After discussing our situation with one of my mentors, I was counseled that the leader *owns* the culture on *any* team. It was the first time that I had heard that phrase, but I certainly now fully understand how true a statement it is. If the leader is pessimistic, the team will be pessimistic. It was clear that Dom and I needed to change our attitudes.

Fortunately, another of Dom's remarkable attributes as a leader was his humility. Despite being brilliant on a number of topics, Dom was a humble man. He would listen. Knowing this, I talked to Dom about the downward spiral. We discussed the team's attitude of pessimism to which we were contributing and, more importantly, how it was sucking the trust and creative juices from the team. Over a handshake, we agreed to help each other curb our negativity and celebrate small victories that were indeed happening. We'd address the challenges but not become mired in them. We agreed to not let anyone hijack the meeting with their negativity.

We were more careful in the words we chose—no more were we uttering sarcastic remarks. We were careful with our body language. No scowling or worried looks. Above all, we focused on staying positive. We'd invest a few minutes before the meeting to think of past successes, however minor, and mention them at the beginning of the meeting. We'd then address the challenges and close each meeting with a reminder, once again, of past successes.

The culture slowly improved. Wins started coming. More wins followed. Within two years, our small team was saving DoD over $100 million annually with no reduction in quality. Our small team was recognized within the industry as a center of excellence in the emerging field of pharmacoeconomics. Our success was nothing less than stunning.

Recall that the leader's optimism gives employees hope that great things are possible from their efforts. Our optimism connected the dots between our collective hard work and the bigger picture—significant cost saving. Our optimism increased the value of the work by making the meaning of the work richer. Optimism grew, as did their confidence and trust in us as leaders.

Dom and I remain very close friends to this day. While our paths don't cross as often as we'd like, we fondly reminisce about this remarkable tour of duty. While there were many reasons for the team's overwhelming success, we unequivocally believe that the turning point was when we agreed to help each other curb our negativity and lead with optimism. We both stuck to our agreement, and great things happened.

Practicing optimism is as complex as it is crucial. It is a delicate balancing act. Leading with pessimism demoralizes, demotivates, and undermines the effectiveness of the entire team. However, blind optimism—or optimism that is not grounded in the reality of the challenges that must be faced—can be just as damaging. This quandary has been coined the "Stockdale Paradox."

James Stockdale was a U.S. Navy vice admiral and aviator awarded the Medal of Honor for his service during the Vietnam War. He had been an American prisoner of war (POW) for over seven years in the notorious Hanoi Hilton.[2] In Jim Collins's classic book *Good to Great*, Jim writes about a conversation he had with Admiral Stockdale regarding his coping strategy during his long confinement in the Vietnamese POW camp. Admiral Stockdale stated, "I never lost faith in the end of the story, I never doubted not only that I would get out, but also that I would prevail in the end and turn the experience into the defining event of my life, which, in retrospect, I would not trade."[3]

When Collins asked who didn't make it out of Vietnam, Admiral Stockdale replied, "Oh, that's easy, the optimists. Oh, they were the ones who said, 'We're going to be out by Christmas.' And Christmas would come, and Christmas would go. Then they'd say, 'We're going to be out by Easter.' And Easter would come, and Easter would go. And then Thanksgiving, and then it would be Christmas again. And they died of a broken heart."[4]

Admiral Stockdale then added, "This is a very important lesson. You must never confuse faith that you will prevail in the end—which you can never afford to lose—with the discipline to confront the most brutal facts of your current reality, whatever they might be." Witnessing this philosophy of duality, Collins went on to describe it as the Stockdale Paradox.[5]

This is indeed a paradox. Leaders who fail to grasp the reality of the challenge, or worse ignore it altogether, will appear naïve and out of touch. Naïve and out-of-touch leaders don't engender confidence. However, if the leader becomes mired in the challenges, they'll create a culture of pessimism, which will demoralize the team.

How does a leader offer a practical approach to this paradox? In his book *Winston Churchill, CEO*, Alan Axelrod offers an explanation: "Churchill was above all else a master mediator, delivering to the world the vision of the reality that confronted it. The genius in this was that the vision always provided hope without for a moment denying peril."[6]

Churchill was the true master in this realm. At arguably England's most tenuous period during World War II, a large remnant of British

Expeditionary Force was successfully evacuated from mainland Europe during what was dubbed the "Miracle at Dunkirk."

During an address to the House of Commons given days after the event, Churchill appropriately acknowledged the heroism displayed by a number of military and civilian units that made the operation a success. These accolades were vitally important to maintaining morale when a land invasion of England by German forces appeared imminent.

However, understanding that he could not for a moment deny the perilous status of the situation and consequently lose credibility with the English people, at the end of the speech Churchill accurately stated, "We must be very careful not to assign to this deliverance the attributes of a victory. Wars are not won by evacuations."

Leaders face the paradox of putting a threat in its appropriate place without paralyzing the masses with fear. Churchill's greatness is that he carefully chose words that found the perfect balance between the two. As such, he tamed the paradox.

All leaders will face this paradox—the need to maintain an air of optimism in the face of significant challenges. The sweet spot is to appropriately address the reality of the situation without negatively impacting morale. To help tame the paradox, find those small victories and celebrate them. Address the challenge, but ensure *you* lead the conversation—choose your words wisely, and don't let anyone hijack the meeting with their negativity.

Another tool a leader can use to tame the paradox—addressing challenges while staying optimistic—is to understand which challenges can be influenced and which cannot. This is a vitally important distinction that, when executed well, ensures the leader is spending their valuable time addressing the right issues. We're busy. No one has time to work on problems that are outside their ability to influence.

In *The 7 Habits of Highly Effective People*, Dr. Stephen Covey writes of the importance of identifying and focusing our time and energy on issues that are within our span of control, which he describes as our "circle of influence."[7] Imagine two concentric circles. The smaller inner circle represents our circle of influence and the larger outside circle our circle of concern. He warns of spending valuable time and energy on issues that certainly are of concern to us but are clearly outside our circle of influence. We have numerous concerns: our boss's mood, traffic, nat-

---

Leadership Lesson

All leaders will face the paradox of exuding optimism in the face of adversity.

Here are some tips:

- Identify what is within your span of control and what is not. Be transparent, and freely communicate this reality to your team.
- Take action on those issues that you can influence.
- Find and celebrate the small victories; discuss them at the beginning and end of meetings.
- Acknowledge the challenges that are outside your span of influence, but don't become mired in them; discuss them in the middle of meetings.
- Don't let anyone hijack or control conversations with their negativity.
- When you sense negativity, don't be a passive participant. Be disciplined—avoid sarcasm and lead with positivity.
- Be mindful of your body language and choice of words. Use words that place the challenge in its appropriate place without creating fear.

---

ural disasters, and bad weather, among a host of others—none of which we have *any* ability to influence. Given that, the logical question is this: Why would we spend any of our valuable time and energy trying to influence these issues?

Covey wisely counsels us to spend time where we can effect change. That is within the smaller inside circle—our "circle of influence." This concept is simple but extremely powerful. I've seen it help others maintain a good attitude in challenging times. In short, it's another powerful tool to tame the Stockdale Paradox. Let me give you three examples.

The first example occurred during one of the most challenging tours of duty of my Navy career. I was placed in charge of a large Navy hospital pharmacy operation with a plethora of problems and extremely low morale and performance. My boss told me that my job was to turn the department around, and quickly.

I knew that a big part of my success would depend on my behaviors, including, of course, my optimism. This tour of duty was immediately after my tour with Dom, which had helped me better appreciate the profound impact that a leader's optimism has on team culture and, ultimately, performance. I knew that, despite the numerous challenges I was facing with this new job, it was imperative that I maintain an optimistic demeanor.

The morale among the twenty or so registered pharmacists who worked for me was especially low. Their pessimism was palpable, and I battled daily to stay positive during the first couple of weeks. There were many times when I felt as though I was losing the battle. I'd retreat to my office for a few minutes each week to regroup when pessimism contaminated my thoughts. Pessimism seemed always to be a wanting companion.

About three weeks into that tour, I scheduled a meeting with all the pharmacists to understand the causes of the low morale. The good news is that they were not shy about sharing their complaints. It was one of the wilder meetings I've ever assembled. Their behavior was boisterous and rowdy. I patiently listened and let them have their day in court.

As the smoke lifted, it appeared that their primary gripe was the distinct difference in pay and benefits among the twenty pharmacists. While all twenty had essentially the same day-to-day job functions, their pay and benefits varied significantly. It was a legitimate complaint. Depending on whether they were an active duty pharmacy officer, a government service pharmacist, or an independently contracted pharmacist—we employed all three types—their pay and benefits differed significantly. At the end of the meeting, I conceded that the pay disparity was a valid concern and that we'd have a follow-up meeting to discuss it further.

I drove home that night with more questions than answers. I knew I needed to get some advice and I talked to one of my mentors, who offered me some words of wisdom: identify what is within your span of control and what is not. That was very good advice. In fact, I had minimal control over the pay and benefits situation. Without delving into the nuances of government employee compensation packages, I was able to offer *some* small pay raises to *some* of those who warranted it, but I could not make the necessary wholesale changes required for their pay and benefits to be truly fair and equitable. I confirmed all this with our human resources department before my next meeting with the twenty pharmacists.

A few days later, we met again. I started the meeting by reaffirming that the pay and benefits situation was indeed unfair. I went on to explain that while I truly wished I could make the necessary changes to make it fair, the truth was that I could not. Despite the fact that many of them understood this, I went into some detail to explain the nuances of the situation. I wanted them to know I had done my homework. I ended by stating I would certainly do what was within my limited span of control to help improve the pay and benefits mismatches, and then I answered their questions.

When all their questions were addressed, I told them that it was important that we now put this issue behind us. I highlighted all the improvements that would be forthcoming to help us do our jobs better (we were refurbishing the entire workflow process). I ended by saying that if, after a period of time, any of them could not let the pay and benefits issue go—if it was simply too difficult for them to accept—I'd understand. However, instead of bringing their unhappiness to work, I asked them to consider moving on. The good news is that, in the end, we didn't lose any pharmacists, and, over a period of a few months, both morale and performance improved significantly.

As my mentor wisely suggested, I distinguished those issues that I could influence from those I could not. I didn't waste an inordinate amount of time and energy addressing the issue of pay and benefits—one that was outside my circle of influence—and I communicated this to the team in an open and honest way. I listened. By stating the facts as they were, I was transparent, which is a powerful way to earn trust. I didn't tell them what they wanted to hear; I told them what they needed to hear. In the end, I was able to tame the paradox: I addressed the challenge without falling into the pit of pessimism.

Another time where I saw the power of this tool work well was while employed as a corporate sales manager after my Navy career. One of my employees, Chuck, an outstanding employee—decisive, an expert in our industry, and just fun to be around—became very agitated when our boss announced a new direction for our sales strategy. Neither of us liked it, and, despite many discussions with the boss, neither of us were able to convince him to change it. For the ensuing week, Chuck stormed into my office a couple of times a day, passionately explaining why it was a stupid decision. His arguments were convincing, especially given that Chuck had more experience in the business than anyone else on the team, including me and the boss.

After that first week, I asked Chuck to come by my office at the end of the day. During our meeting, I told Chuck that I agreed with all his arguments regarding why he disagreed with the boss's decision. I went on to say that, unfortunately, that decision had been made. We both agreed that there was *no way* to convince the boss to change his mind. There was *nothing* we could do about it. It was done—that train had left the station.

I then drew two concentric circles on a piece of paper. I explained the two circles—the smaller inner circle being the circle of influence, the larger outer circle the circle of concern. While he had legitimate concerns about this decision, as I did, there was *nothing* either one of us could do about it. It was clearly in the circle of concern. He needed to let it go and focus his time and energy on issues that he *could* influence. I finished by saying that I absolutely loved working with him and how valuable he was to the team. However, if he could not get beyond this issue, it was probably better for him to move on, as his ongoing griping was infecting others, including me! I clearly stated that I wanted him to stay, but it was important for him to accept this decision. I asked him to think about it that evening and let me know his thoughts in the morning.

The next morning, Chuck burst into my office with a wide smile and excitedly told me how he'd been thinking about the circles all night long. He now understood clearly that the boss's decision was well outside his ability to influence. It was done, and he was good with it. More importantly, Chuck went on to tell me that he thought about the concept of what he could influence and what he could not in the context of a litany of other personal issues that he had been wrestling with. He could now see that many of these issues were well beyond his ability to change. He explained that when that became clear to him, it was as if a large burden had been lifted from his shoulders. Chuck and I remain close friends to this day and often reminisce about that day. He almost always tells me of other examples in his life when he was able to let go of issues when he understood that they were clearly outside of his control.

Once again, in this example, I chose not to waste time and energy addressing a poor decision that was not going to be changed. While it was a concern, it was clearly outside my ability to influence. Additionally, as with my first example, I explained this to Chuck in an open and honest way. I listened. By stating the facts as they were, I was transparent, which created more trust between us. I was able to tame the paradox: I addressed a challenge while staying positive.

My last story regarding this powerful tool occurred a few years ago at a leadership seminar that I was giving to a group of naval officers at Walter Reed National Military Medical Center in Bethesda, Maryland. During the seminar, I included a section on optimism. At the end of the workshop, a participant asked me a great question.

She explained that she understood why a leader needs to be optimistic. However, she led a small team of nurses who often complained about the terrible parking situation at the hospital—staff sometimes had to walk twenty to twenty-five minutes from the staff parking area to work. She asked, "How do you put a happy face on that?"

It was a great question. I told her that I had worked at that same hospital twenty-five years earlier. During my tour there, I was placed on a small team that was tasked to identify, via survey, the top morale issues among hospital staff. Interestingly, the number-one morale issue at that time was inadequate staff parking. Half-jokingly but half-seriously, I went on to say that I'd wager a bet that parking would be the number-one issue at that hospital twenty-five years from now.

I then advised her to be honest and transparent when discussing this with her staff. Acknowledge it as a legitimate concern. Parking *is* a problem. However, while it's a concern, there is nothing you can do to improve it. I went on to say that I'd consider describing these long walks to and from the parking area as opportunities for some physical fitness. Bring comfortable shoes and enjoy the exercise! In the same conversation, I'd consider mentioning the advantages of working at that hospital, of which there were many. Acknowledge the parking issue, but don't become mired in it.

Napoleon's famous quote uttered over two hundred years ago—"A leader is a dealer in hope"—still rings true today. Optimism spreads enthusiasm, hope, confidence, and trust. Given that, how damaging is the cynicism, doubt, negativity, and fear spewed by a pessimistic leader? Is it accurate to say that a pessimistic leader is more harmful than an absent leader?

I ask this question at many of my seminars. When I do, I carefully watch the body language of my audience. Universally, regardless of country or culture, heads nod in agreement. Participants agree that a pessimistic leader causes more harm than an absent leader. Those thoughts are always verified during the follow-on discussion. The fact is *no one* wants to work for a pessimist.

Let's use a hypothetical example: Jim, the new leader of a small sales team, has been on the job for a few weeks and has maintained a pleasant and upbeat demeanor. No angry outbursts. No incivility. He's been appropriately encouraging, cheerful, and positive. The household move to the new area was uneventful, and the family is adjusting well. The team is hitting their targets. Jim's boss is happy. From Jim's perspective, all is going well.

However, after a few more weeks, the honeymoon period begins to fade. The sales team isn't hitting their targets consistently. Jim's boss is asking more difficult and probing questions. Jim's wife is having difficulty finding work. Jim's beginning to feel the pressure, and it's affecting his sleep. Jim worked on Saturday and missed his twelve-year-old daughter's volleyball game. While he had planned to join his wife on the following Monday to help chaperone a school field trip, he abruptly cancels those plans and puts in a full day of work. He feels the pressure to put more hours in. He begins to feel both resentful and guilty. Jim knows he needs to recharge his batteries and vainly vows to carve out more family time next month.

On that Monday morning—the same Monday that he was supposed to be on the field trip with his wife and daughter—Jim is meeting with his sales team. Jim's finance director reports that the team's travel budget will be cut another 10 percent for the quarter. Jim instinctively responds with an outburst that surprises the team. Everyone in the meeting stops talking. They collectively look down at their cell phones and shift nervously in their seats.

Leadership Lesson

A pessimistic leader causes more harm than an absent leader.

Leaders have three choices:

1. Be optimistic.
2. Fake it.
3. Don't show up.

If this has ever happened to you—it has certainly happened to me— you know that you immediately realize that your outburst has put everyone on edge. However, the damage is done. In this case, Jim just caused more harm by showing up than if he had simply taken the day off.

Does a pessimistic leader cause more harm than an absent leader? Absolutely. Given this, leaders have three choices: (1) be optimistic, (2) fake it, or (3) don't show up. Pessimism simply has no place in leadership.

This second choice, "faking it," elicits much dialogue in my seminars. Sometimes participants will argue that leaders will lose credibility with their team if they fake it. I disagree.

History is replete with examples of leaders successfully faking optimism in times of challenge and despair. One example occurred in July 1942. General Dwight Eisenhower was promoted to lieutenant general and named to head Operation Torch, the Allied invasion of French North Africa during World War II. In front of his immediate staff, General Eisenhower maintained an air of confidence and optimism throughout the campaign. As D-Day for the invasion drew near, Eisenhower continued to be the picture of confidence. In reality, he was irritable and often depressed, smoking up to *four* packs of Camel cigarettes a day.

On the eve of the invasion, General Eisenhower wrote a fascinating communiqué to his boss, General George Marshall. In it Eisenhower candidly admitted that "it has been a trifle difficult to keep up, in front of everybody, a proper attitude of confidence and optimism."[8] In his captivating book on the Operation Torch campaign, Rick Atkinson accurately captures the true meaning of that short communiqué when he writes, "For now, the concealment of General Eisenhower's anxieties was part of the art of leadership."[9]

In other words, Eisenhower was faking it. More importantly, Atkinson accurately describes faking optimism as something a leader sometimes has to do in order to succeed.

How does a leader maintain an air of optimism in the vortex of life's hurricanes? Sometimes a leader needs to fake it. You won't lose credibility if you do. In my experience and research, given the immeasurable harm pessimism brings to team performance, a leader has no choice but to be optimistic. Succumbing to pessimism is simply not a viable option.

One key aspect of fostering optimism in the workplace for yourself and your subordinates is to promote a healthy work-life balance.

One of the most difficult challenges I wrestled with throughout my Navy career was balancing my time, energy, and focus on being the best naval officer I could be with other important aspects of my life—namely, my growing family, my desire to exercise, and time for prayer. As my jobs became more complex and demanding, finding that balance became much more challenging. When my life was not in balance—namely, when I worked long hours, missed family events, and neglected exercise and prayer—it nagged at me. I'd get bitter that the job was sucking an inordinate amount of time and energy out of me. A perfect example was when I missed our eldest daughter's high school volleyball games because of an "important" meeting. I still remember the feeling of guilt that would quietly haunt me, especially when I'd miss family events repeatedly. When I neglected important aspects of my life in favor of work, maintaining a good attitude, and certainly staying optimistic, was much more difficult. When I felt that my life was more in balance, being optimistic came much easier. It was extremely difficult to fake optimism when I was bitter.

What can a leader do to find the elusive balance? Be mindful. Be mindful of your loved ones. Be mindful of your interests and passions outside of work. Each leader must find their own unique solution to this conundrum. My ideal work-life balance will be different from someone else's and so forth. The key is to remain mindful that we need to constantly strive to find that balance.

During my Navy career, I missed some family events and made others. I did not find the perfect balance, nor have I met anyone who has. However, along the way, I did learn a simple but powerful tip that helped me maintain a sense of balance. I learned it many years ago when I saw it put into practice during an important meeting, and I have tried to use it ever since. What's the practice? If your spouse, child, or anyone close to you calls you while you're at work, unless you're in an absolutely *mission critical* situation, take the call. Let me tell you how I learned this particular pearl of wisdom.

I had just been selected to be a member of the hospital board of directors and was at my first board meeting. I was nervous and intimidated as I fidgeted with my pencil and notebook. I scanned the room and realized that I was the most junior officer present. The other officers sitting around the large, imposing oak table were senior naval officers and had many years of experience. As the newest member of this august group, I was attending my very first C-suite-level meeting.

With all members of the board of directors sitting at their assigned seats, at exactly eight o'clock sharp that morning, the commanding officer entered the room. We instinctively jumped to attention as someone in the group loudly announced, "Attention on deck!" While this was standard protocol with which I was very familiar, the episode caused more butterflies in my stomach.

The task of this group was to run the hospital as envisioned by the CO. While I knew this was important work, how the CO and the team conducted business was a mystery to me. Although this took place many years ago, I still vividly remember something the CO did during that meeting that left a profound and lasting impression on me.

About ten minutes into the one-hour scheduled meeting, the CO's secretary entered the room and informed him that his wife had just called. While it wasn't urgent, the secretary wanted to let him know. (This was in the era before cell phones.) The CO thanked her, excused himself, and headed for the door. As he left the room, he told us to continue the conversation and that he'd get briefed on what he missed. He told us that he was going to call his wife back.

I was taken aback. Perplexed, I wondered why he had abruptly left such an important meeting. It certainly didn't fit my preconceived notions of a commanding officer's behavior. I looked around the table to get confirmation that others were similarly surprised by the CO's sudden departure. They weren't. The conversation continued without skipping a beat. This was clearly not the first time the CO had left a meeting to return a routine call from his wife. Over the ensuing year or so, I learned that this was indeed the case. In fact, the CO similarly left meetings to return calls from his children.

What was the impact of this unexpected behavior?

All members of the command loved him for it. Morale under his leadership was always high. We had great confidence in him, and we worked very hard for him. The command enjoyed enormous success. More importantly, he appeared to have a loving wife and family.

I, along with my peers, greatly appreciated the CO's modeling of a healthy work-life balance. It encouraged us to do the same. This subtle but extremely powerful message showed that he cared for his family, and it showed that he cared for us. Like I said, we all loved him, trusted him, and worked extremely hard for him, and the command enjoyed abundant success.

Recall that the behaviors of the leader are generally emulated. Not surprisingly, this is true in the case of modeling a healthy work-life balance. Leaders who maintain this balance quietly set that as an example for others to emulate. Employees who pratice a healthy work-life balance tend to have better relationships with bosses and coworkers. They feel a greater sense of control over their lives. They are generally able to manage work issues while at work, and not while at home. The opposite is also generally true—they manage family issues at home, and not while at work. They're more motivated, have less conflict, and are more productive. Leaders who enjoy a healthy work-life balance help create healthy organizations that foster a culture of trust and high performance.

Recently, a boss wrote a letter to her employees regarding her expectations for working parents on the work-life balance issue, and it became a viral Facebook post. Charity Delmo, the founder and managing director of a company called Ideal Visa Consultancy, wrote the following letter to her employees:[10]

Dear Employees,

I hired you in the hope that you can be a good provider to your family, not to take you away from them, to give you additional skills, not take your parental skills away from your kids, to make you a better person, not just for the company but all the more for your family.

So, when the time comes that you will have to choose between attending your sons and daughters' school activities over a client's needs, if you have to choose between your wife or your husband's needs over mine as your boss—please choose them.

You see, not all employers will understand some of my principles in leadership but I would rather close this company than seeing you miss your kids school activities because you have to be in a meeting, or seeing you getting broken because of your unfixed misunderstanding with your husband or wife. They are your home first before the company gave you a second home, they're your family before you became mine.

I have always believed that a person who's happy at home is also happy at work.

So, go home. Be home.

Your work can wait. I can wait.

Your family, the home that you built, once broken, will never be the same again. You will never be the same again.

Love,

Boss

Controversial? Over the top? Some would argue that it is. I don't. I imagine these employees were thrilled to read this letter. The question that needs to be answered is this: Are workers who are happy with their work-family balance more engaged, committed, and productive than other workers? Researchers from around the world have been hard at work studying and surveying this issue for decades. What did they find? Unequivocally, companies that practiced family-friendly policies benefited with improved commitment, engagement, and performance. These improvements were attributable to reduced turnover, absenteeism, and stress.

The following sample of studies show that family-friendly policies improve company performance:

- Fortune 500 firms found that announcements of work-life initiatives were associated with increased shareholder returns: some $60 million per initiative, per firm. The author argues that once a work-life practice becomes normalized, it signals the market that the company is more desirable.[11]
- Thirty-six pharmaceutical companies in the United States found

that the use of flexible work hours can have a real effect on performance: an increase of some 10 percent in firm productivity.[12]

- Researchers found that family-friendly policies are associated with higher commitment to the organization and reduced turnover and retention problems.[13]
- Analysis of 527 U.S. companies found that firms with a wider range of work-life practices had greater performance, profit-sales growth, and organizational performance.[14]
- Researchers found that work-life conflict contributes to reduced work effort and performance and increased absenteeism and turnover.[15]

Leaders need to be upbeat and optimistic. When your work-life balance is out of sync, that becomes much more challenging. Further, other team members are watching and emulating what you do. When the leader's work-life balance becomes visibly sidetracked, employees' work-life balance will more likely get sidetracked, all of which will result in reduced commitment and performance.

Understandably, there will be times when the team will need to put in long hours. However, such periods should be the exception, not the rule.

As mentioned, throughout my Navy career I tried very hard to find the optimal work-life balance with my family. There were other areas, in addition to my family, where I found this challenging: exercise and prayer.

There are many things I love about the military, and one of them is the rigid requirement to maintain your physical fitness. If you don't meet the standards, you're processed out of the military. That requirement to meet physical fitness standards begins from day one of your military career.

Part of the lengthy process to join the U.S. Armed Forces is completion of a thorough physical examination. When I began the process to join the military all those years ago, I had no concerns about passing the physical exam. I had always been physically active and played a number of sports. So when I jumped on the scale in the Navy recruiting office and found that I was twenty pounds overweight, I was shocked and embarrassed. I realized that I had gotten away from working out on a routine basis the past couple of years and my physical inactivity had caught up with me. The bottom line was that I needed to lose the twenty pounds in order to get into the Navy. I vowed to lose it as soon as possible. I also vowed to never get so out of shape again. Over the next few weeks, I worked extremely hard—running, lifting weights, eating healthy—and lost the weight. After an auspicious start, my Navy adventure began.

More importantly, I kept my vow to stay in good physical condition. I maintained a regular schedule of physical fitness throughout my thirty-year career and still do today. While in the Navy, my routine was to exercise during lunch. In addition to keeping the weight off, I used that time to muse over complex issues. I often tell people that I'm not a big idea kind of leader. However, the few good ideas I did cook up during my Navy career all came during physical exercise. I could find clarity on complex issues when I was exercising. This was especially true when I had pending nonjudicial punishment proceedings, or "Captain's Masts" in Navy jargon, that I'd have to preside over.[16] These were rarely clear-cut—there were always ample gray areas to navigate. More importantly, physical exercise helped me maintain a positive attitude. Knowing all this, no matter how taxing the job, and they got pretty taxing toward the end of my career, my commitment to maintaining an exercise routine never wavered.

Did I find excuses not to work out? Absolutely. Fatigue and a hectic schedule were the most common. I learned from others a few tricks to get moving: Take ten minutes to go for a walk. Use the stairs instead of the elevator. If you travel a lot, bring a deck of cards and do a deck of cards workout in your hotel room—they're great workouts, and you can knock one out in twenty minutes. Simply make a commitment to get moving.

During those times when I missed my exercise routine because of the overwhelming burden of work, I found it much more difficult to remain upbeat. Optimism came easier to me when I exercised. Indeed, studies have found a clear relationship between exercise, cognition, and optimism:

- Research shows that previously sedentary adults who undertook an aerobic fitness plan for six months boosted their cognition.[17]

- One German study that tracked four thousand people older than fifty-five for two years found that those who rarely took part in physical activities were more than twice as likely to suffer from a cognitive impairment by the end of the study than those who engaged in exercise such as gardening, swimming, or cycling a few times a week.[18]
- A study found that schoolchildren in New York who were in the top 5 percent of the fitness rankings scored 36 percentile points higher on standardized academic tests than students in the bottom 5 percent.[19]
- Exercise has been found to spur the release of such neurotransmitters as serotonin, noradrenaline, and dopamine, which help regulate signaling in the brain. These neurotransmitters are similar to those released by antidepressants.[20]

In addition to physical exercise, as a Christian, prayer and being part of a religious community is an important component of my life. Especially during my command tour, when I wrestled mightily with that elusive work-life balance, this aspect of my life helped me maintain an upbeat demeanor. Interestingly, a Pew Research study found that regular participation in a religious community was clearly linked to higher levels of happiness.[21] In addition, prayer and faith was a way for me to ask for help with complex issues and to slow down the decision-making process. I made better decisions when I took the time to pray on them.

Throughout my Navy career, I always made an effort to spend time with my family, remain physically fit, pray, have faith as a Christian, and be part of a religious community. When my work-life balance regarding these important aspects of my life were out of sync—when I chose to neglect them because of the overwhelming burden of work—I found it much more difficult to remain upbeat. I cannot overstate the enormous return on investment from the time spent on these activities. They helped me maintain my physical, emotional, and spiritual health; find clarity on complex issues; and optimize decision making. Optimism came easier to me and I was a more effective leader when I spent time with my family, exercised, prayed, and was part of a religious community. I counsel leaders to find some pursuit or interest of supreme importance in which they can find solace.

Leadership Lesson

Without energy and health, it's difficult to be optimistic. Be mindful of maintaining work-life balance, and always strive to optimize it by prioritizing your loved ones, interests, and passions outside of work.

- If a loved one calls while you're at work, unless the place is on fire, take the call.
- When the boss's work-life balance is in sync, employees' work-life balance will more likely be in sync. The boss subtly gives employees permission to enjoy time with loved ones without guilt.
- Workers who are happy with their work-family balance are more engaged, committed, and productive in their work.
- Physical fitness improves brain function and produces the same neurotransmitters as antidepressant medications.

In my readings I came across a quote that perfectly encapsulates this conundrum. I refer to it often in my seminars. The quote is this: "Without energy and health, it is often difficult to be optimistic."[22] When we are more mindful of this truth, and when we understand the importance of maintaining optimism when in a leadership position, we'll make a greater effort to find an optimal work–life balance.

The leader's optimism gives employees hope that great things are possible from their efforts. It connects the dots between hard work and the bigger picture, clarifies the purpose of work, and increases the value of the work. When the meaning of work is richer, the result is a fertile environment to grow trust. In the end, the leader's optimism inspires trust.

KEY POINTS

1. A leader's optimism gives others hope that great things are possible from their efforts.
2. Teams led by pessimistic leaders underperform in the fog of malaise, helplessness, and passivity; they're easily overwhelmed by even a meager challenge.
3. Great leaders know that pessimism is poison. Its lethality lies in its insidious infectiousness.
4. All leaders will face the paradox of exuding optimism in the face of adversity. Here are some tips:
   - Identify what is within your span of control and what is not. Be transparent, and freely communicate this reality to your team.
   - Take action on those issues that you can influence.
   - Find and celebrate the small victories; discuss them at the beginning and end of meetings.
   - Acknowledge the challenges that are outside your span of influence, but don't become mired in them; discuss them in the middle of meetings.
   - Don't let anyone hijack or control conversations with their negativity.
   - When you sense negativity, don't be a passive participant. Be disciplined—avoid sarcasm and lead with positivity.
   - Be mindful of your body language and choice of words. Use words that place the challenge in its appropriate place without creating fear.
5. A pessimistic leader causes more harm than an absent leader. Leaders have three choices: be optimistic, fake it, or don't show up.
6. Without energy and health, it's difficult to be optimistic. Be mindful of maintaining work-life balance, and always strive to optimize it by prioritizing your loved ones, interests, and passions outside of work.
   - If a loved one calls while you're at work, unless the place is on fire, take the call.
   - When the boss's work-life balance is in sync, employees'

work-life balance will more likely be in sync. The boss subtly gives employees permission to enjoy time with loved ones without guilt.

- Workers who are happy with their work-family balance are more engaged, committed, and productive in their work.
- Physical fitness improves brain function and produces the same neurotransmitters as antidepressant medications.

9

CONTINUOUSLY LEARN THE ART OF LEADERSHIP

Intellectual growth should commence at birth and cease only at death.

—Albert Einstein

Throughout the book we've discussed how, as leaders, monitoring our behaviors is the key to earning trust, building teams, and creating organizational excellence. Team members are watching us, and they will emulate our behaviors. Our behaviors create the team culture, and team culture dictates team performance. When we go out of our way to build relationships with our team members, their trust in us increases, and people work harder when they trust their boss.

Why did I devote a chapter to discussing the importance of continuously learning the art of leadership? It's a short chapter but an extremely important one. By continuously learning the art of leadership, we'll be reminded of the profound importance of our behaviors. We'll more likely act in a caring way, especially when challenges arise. Likewise, we'll more likely proactively find opportunities to capitalize on the hundreds of interactions we have with our employees each day. These are behaviors that need to be learned and refined. By continuously learning the art of leadership, we'll more likely practice it in our day-to-day life.

In the beginning of my speaking career, I was asked a question that I struggled to answer. I was bothered by the answer I gave, which prompted me to research the topic of the query. Fortunately, I'm much better prepared now to answer that question.

The question was this: Why don't more leaders practice these behaviors?

It's a great question. Given that a recent Center for Creative Leadership study found that 38 percent of new chief executives fail in their first eighteen months on the job, it's an important one.[1]

Harvard Business Review published a study that helps answer the question.[2] The study identified a very common barrier that bedevils companies struggling to change their culture: leaders don't commit to necessary changes in their own behavior.

Why not? Some leaders don't appreciate that *all* their behaviors on a week-by-week, day-by-day, hour-by-hour, minute-by-minute, and second-by-second basis either increase or decrease their employees' confidence in their ability to lead. As leaders, our behaviors engender either more trust or, worse, fear, and team performance will either soar or suffer. Even for those leaders who *do* appreciate this strong correlation, disciplining our behaviors is challenging, and even more so when life gets stressful. It's much easier to harness our behaviors when everything is going well and far harder when we hit a rough patch.

How can we remind ourselves of this strong correlation between our behaviors, culture, and team performance? More importantly, how can we increase the likelihood of employing the behaviors discussed in this book? By continuously learning the art of leadership.

Much of what we, as leaders, are responsible for lies outside our direct span of control. To bring this point to life, during my seminars I often ask participants—all of whom are leaders with varying degrees of responsibility—how much control they have over what is happening at this moment back at their places of work. Of course, the answer is they have very little control. Likewise, on any day of the week, leaders have much less control over what is happening in the trenches than they imagine. On the other hand, what *do* leaders control? What do we *always*

Leadership Lesson

Through continued study, leaders will better appreciate the profound influence of their behaviors. Leaders will then more likely behave in ways that earn trust.

control? More explicitly, what do we *always* control that has a *profound* impact on how our team actually performs in the trenches? Our behaviors. *We control our behaviors 100 percent of the time.* As discussed in chapter 8, harnessing our behaviors lies within our span of influence. When I fully understood this concept—that my behaviors were within my span of influence *and* had a profound impact on team performance—I put much more energy, effort, and focus on monitoring my behaviors rather than focusing on results.

Did I make mistakes? Absolutely. While in command, I recall losing my temper in a very public forum when doling out punishment to a staff member during a formal Captain's Mast proceeding. I was very frustrated, and my growing frustration caused me to explode in anger during the proceedings. I crossed the line and humiliated the staff member. I immediately regretted it, but the damage was done.

What helped me to become more disciplined? I read books and articles, observed and talked with other leaders, and attended leadership development workshops when my schedule permitted. Please review my list of recommended books listed in the "Appendix: Recommended Reading" section. Each book had a profound impact on me and helped shape me as a leader. The more I read, the more I came to appreciate the importance of continuously learning the art of leadership. I was constantly reminded of the profound influence of my behaviors. Consequently, when faced with a challenging situation, especially during a vulnerable time when life was a bit messy and my stress level was peaking, I was better prepared to react appropriately. *You* are now better prepared when you face *your* crucible moments. More broadly, I'm hopeful that this book has been a means to, as Einstein wrote, perpetuate "intellectual growth" on the topic of leadership.

I invite you to continue your growth by signing up for my monthly leadership blogs and podcasts on my website at www.broukerleadership-solutions.com.

KEY POINT

Through continued study, leaders will better appreciate the profound influence of their behaviors. Leaders will more likely behave in ways that earn trust.

10

LEADING IN CRISIS

It's hard to lead people when you've lost control.

—Marshall Goldsmith

Leadership is never more important than in times of crisis, whether minor or not-so-minor. Every organization at some time will face a crisis. They come in all sizes and often are completely unexpected. The only known is that they *will* come. What should a leader do to prepare for this inevitability?

Of course, it's essential that leaders proactively create contingency plans for the next crisis by identifying vulnerable areas, analyzing the organization's state of readiness, providing appropriate staff training, staging crisis readiness simulations, and updating/creating a crisis response plan. However, there is a famous military maxim that says, "Every plan is a good one—until the first shot is fired." In large part, organizations will either weather the storm well or not based on what leaders do *before* the first shots are fired.

Whether in crisis mode or otherwise, as discussed throughout this book, team culture is a byproduct of the team leader. More specifically, the leader's behaviors create either an environment of calm or an environment of unease. Further, trust is earned exponentially faster in the former case as compared to the latter. In other words, leaders who generally lead with care and compassion—leaders who know their staff, don't ignore good or poor performance, continuously learn the art of leadership, and are visible, respectful, and optimistic—will create calm and more easily earn trust. Leaders who generally lead with command and control, however, tend to create cultures of unease, and trust is more difficult to attain. This is not to say that these leaders are uncaring—they simply don't make relationship building with team members a priority. Unquestionably, in times of crisis—when there is great uncertainty— those organizations that proactively build trust up and down the chain of command will weather the storm much better than those that do not.

A few months prior to the publication of this book, I had two very different experiences that helped me better understand the profound importance of proactively building trust. One experience had to do with the coronavirus crisis. In early March 2020, I visited the frontline health-care providers at EvergreenHealth Medical Center in Seattle, Washington. At that time, they were *the* epicenter of the crisis in the United States. I watched in admiration as the health-care team carefully provided high-level inpatient medical care to very ill patients infected with the virus. The other experience was some stunning information I learned while reading a book during the time of my EvergreenHealth visit on Continental Army leadership during the American Revolutionary War. You must be thinking—how could these two things possibly be related?

Let me start with my visit to EvergreenHealth. Well before *coronavirus* became a household term, the senior leaders at EvergreenHealth quietly and steadfastly worked to prepare for this type of emergency. Of course, like all reputable hospitals, they provided appropriate training for their staff on emergency preparedness. However, the leaders at this hospital—perhaps to a greater extent than at most hospitals—did much more to prepare. What did they do?

Due to a change in leadership, in the months leading up to the pandemic, the leadership team formed the habit of walking around the hospital and engaging with the employees. They made more of an effort to get to know a little about each of them. They proactively made them-

---

Leadership Lesson

In times of crisis—when there is great uncertainty—those organizations that proactively build trust up and down the chain of command will weather the storm much better than those that do not.

selves visible and listened to their employees' concerns. They became more engaged leaders—and more approachable leaders.

Over time, because of these hundreds of seemingly innocuous exchanges, these leaders built stronger relationships with their team members. What happened? A culture of mutual respect and collaboration was created. In short, trust grew up and down the chain of command.

Then, unexpectedly, the coronavirus appeared on the world stage. Suddenly infected patients arrived at the hospital. Literally overnight, the staff at EvergreenHealth was treating a host of very ill people—the first hospital in the United States to treat a mass influx of coronavirus-infected patients. How did the hospital team perform? Exceedingly well. The initial contact with the virus was intense and difficult, but the team was never overwhelmed. They made—and continue to make—excellent patient care decisions at every level and work bravely and unselfishly to provide the best care possible.

The bottom line is that over time—several months before a crisis hit—the leaders created high morale, and, when a crisis hit, the team performed at an extraordinary level. This was the deciding factor that allowed the EvergreenHealth team to meet the challenge. In fact, a visiting health-care professional leading a team from an internationally recognized health-care organization sent the following email to the team leaders: "I was amazed at how much the team was able to accomplish in such a quick period of time. I learned a lot from my time with your team and I think you'll probably quickly find that your group will set the national example for how to get this [proper diagnosis and treatment of coronavirus patients] done as effectively as possible." (As an example, among many firsts, the EvergreenHealth team established the first successful drive-through coronavirus testing site in the country.)

What could the EvergreenHealth story possibly have to do with Continental Army leadership during the American Revolutionary War? Actually, a lot.

A book that I happened to be reading at the time of my visit to EvergreenHealth was *Contest for Liberty: Military Leadership in the Continental Army*. One striking fact I learned while reading this book is that over the span of the eight-year Revolutionary War (1775–1783), members of the Continental Army were rarely paid, fed, or clothed on a regular basis. Because of this—and not surprisingly—some units simply refused to fight. They committed mutiny. Why did some units fight while others chose not to? It depended on unit leadership. Those units that believed their leaders cared for their well-being did fight; those that did not chose not to fight.

Interestingly, before the Revolutionary War battles raged, the Continental Army leaders whose units chose to fight practiced the exact same leadership techniques as the EvergreenHealth leaders. Continental Army leaders were visible leaders—they walked around the campsites and talked with their soldiers. They made an effort to get to know a little about each of them and listened to their concerns. They were engaged leaders—and approachable leaders.

The fact is that *all* organizations will face crises. Whether a novel infectious disease that suddenly appears on the world stage or the chaos of military battle, the next crisis for your organizational could be around the corner. Great leaders prepare for this inevitability by proactively building relationships with their team members. Trust improves and the team performs better. Whether a soldier in the eighteenth century or a health-care provider in the twenty-first century, when people know their leader cares for them, they'll deliver.

Now let's turn our attention to what a leader should do after the crisis hits.

Earlier this year, when it was becoming clear that coronavirus would be a serious threat, Kim Scott, a workplace consultant, wrote the following in a *Wall Street Journal* article: "Everyone will remember how their boss responded during this time."[1]

Kim is absolutely correct. At any time—in crisis mode or otherwise—all behaviors of the leader mold team morale. However, during a crisis, the behaviors of the leader have *enormous* influence. As such, turbulent times are tremendous opportunities for leaders to influence morale—and consequently improve trust and team performance—in profound ways. While some behaviors are more impactful than others, there are a few that have an inordinate impact.

The first thing a leader needs to do in a crisis is get as many pertinent facts about the situation as quickly as possible. Truth is difficult to find at any time, but much more difficult in the fog of a crisis. Verify sources. Without clarity, you may respond in a way that wastes time and valuable

Leadership Lesson

During a crisis, the behaviors of the leader have enormous influence.

resources. In addition to optimizing decision making, having facts will help build credibility with your staff.

While deployed onboard the USNS *Comfort* to the Caribbean Sea in 1994 as part of Operation Uphold Democracy, our mission suddenly changed from a humanitarian mission to a military intervention.[2] While we were anticipating minimal casualties among the 25,000 U.S. troops involved in the operation, the medical supplies needed to support an armed intervention are much different from those needed to support a humanitarian mission. The crew was uneasy with this change, primarily because we were unsure whether we could provide adequate medical support for this new mission. The ship's commanding officer, Captain Charles Blankenship, calmly asked all department heads to immediately provide data regarding our respective ability to support the new mission. After crunching the numbers, he held a series of Captain's Calls (Navy jargon for town hall meetings) where he calmly told us in a few words that we were indeed mission capable. He then opened the meeting up to questions. What was fascinating to me was how quickly the mood in the room went from unease to "we can do this!" In a crisis, the first thing you need to do is collect facts.

A crucial next step is to get in front of your team, just as Captain Blankenship did. This can be done either live (best) or via synchronous (good) or asynchronous (OK) webinar. Either way, simply being visible can reduce uncertainty and anxiety—it builds trust. Get the facts, report them, and then turn it over for questions. Genuinely listen to your team members' concerns. You don't need to have all the answers. Sheryl Sandberg famously wrote, "True leadership stems from individuality that is honest and sometimes imperfectly expressed . . . leaders should strive for authenticity over perfection."[3] She is absolutely correct—you'll *never* have all the answers. That's OK—the team will benefit enormously from your mere presence. You'll be much more authentic—and build much more trust—by admitting you don't know an answer rather than pretending you do.

Recall my story in chapter 5 about the power of being visible. When I was in command at Naval Hospital Bremerton, I spent about three hours or so meeting with a large group of employees addressing a topic that was of grave concern to them: possible layoffs for all four hundred. Never at *any* time during those three meetings did I provide value-added information; I was not able to provide a solid answer to a single question. Nevertheless, they ended up trusting me significantly more than all other groups in the command, and, amazingly, many within the group perceived that I actually *did* answer their inquiries.

While I certainly didn't provide any concrete answers, what I tried to do at these meetings, as well during other interactions, was have the facts, listen to people's concerns, remain calm, and be honest and optimistic.

In their book *The Leader's Bookshelf*, Admiral James Stavridis and Manning Ancell surveyed more than two hundred active and retired four-star military officers regarding their favorite leadership books. The authors then assembled their responses to identify the top fifty books, most of which dealt with leading in crisis. Reviewing these fifty books in depth, they concluded that two common leadership behaviors emerged that were essential to successfully navigating a crisis: being calm and being optimistic. Recall that employees generally emulate the behaviors of the leader. This is especially true in a crisis. How the leader behaves is how team members will behave. The leader needs to show a steady hand, an optimistic smile, and a calm disposition. When in the tempest, people need to remain calm and hopeful. The leader needs to show that calm resolve and provide that hope.

In my experience, the best leaders I worked for remained calm under *all* conditions. For a leader, the importance of calmness under fire is impossible to overstate. When the crisis hits, people have a natural tendency to become agitated, even panic. They begin to question the decision making of their leaders. These reactions produce everything the organization doesn't need in times of crisis—inefficiency, disunity, and dismay. The leader who remains calm is the one who can rally and unify the troops when they need it most.

Whether carrying out a mass casualty operation onboard the USNS *Comfort* during the Persian Gulf War, dealing with a potential shutdown of an intensive care unit due to a labor dispute, or preparing for the immediate departure of your C-suite team due to operational needs, leading with calmness will help improve your ability to focus on the right things, at the right time, and in the right way. It will allow you to better communicate your needs to other people and help you make more effective, intelligent, and emotion-free decisions.

The only other choice a leader has is to *not* remain calm—you can get angry. While it's okay to feel anger, it's not okay to lead with it. Anger runs counter to every positive effect that leaders should try to create in their teams—confidence, cohesion, and commitment. All these are the very elements needed to solve the complex problems encountered in a crisis. An angry leader will stifle creativity, and employees will hesitate to bring problems forward. The leader will be less informed and consequently less likely to make good decisions. History has numerous examples of calamitous events occurring when teams lack creativity, confidence, cohesion, and commitment: Chernobyl. Watergate. The Tenerife air disaster.

Let's turn to the importance of showing optimism in a crisis. While

---

Leadership Lessons

The five key behaviors a leader must employ during a crisis are:

1. Get as many pertinent facts about the crisis as quickly as possible.
2. Be visible. Get in front of your people. Listen to their concerns. Schedule these events with some regularity.
3. Be honest. Tell them what they need to hear, not what they want to hear.
4. Be calm. Show a steady hand, a confident smile, and a calm disposition.
5. Be optimistic. Bring hope by creating a vision for life after the crisis passes.

optimism is an essential behavior for leaders in all situations—and especially in a crisis—the optimism must be framed in realism. While the
leader must be optimistic, he must also be honest. In a crisis, people
want—and deserve—the truth. Don't tell them what they want to hear;
tell them what they need to hear. How does a leader walk this knife's
edge of optimism and honesty?

Recall the quote from Admiral James Stockdale regarding this
conundrum: "This is a very important lesson. You must never confuse
faith that you will prevail in the end—which you can never afford to
lose—with the discipline to confront the most brutal facts of your current
reality, whatever they might be."

As we discussed in chapter 8 when we talked about optimism, one
way to effectively deal with this challenge when in a crisis is to determine
what is within your ability to control and what is not. Again, the logical
question is this: Why would we spend precious time and energy concerning ourselves with anything we cannot control? Try to disregard the
items that are outside of your control—and there will be many. Instead,
focus on that which you *do* control. What we *do* control are our behaviors, and that is where our focus should be. How we *behave* during the
crisis will directly influence how our team will *perform* during the crisis.

In summary, here are the five key behaviors a leader must employ
during a crisis:

1. Get as many pertinent facts about the crisis as quickly as possible.
2. Be visible. Get in front of your people. Listen to their concerns.
   Schedule these events with some regularity.
3. Be honest. Tell them what they need to hear, not what they
   want to hear.
4. Be calm. Show a steady hand, a confident smile, and a calm
   disposition.
5. Be optimistic. Bring hope by creating a vision for life after the
   crisis passes.

During times of crisis, all behaviors of the leader have a significant
impact on culture. Morale is fickle, and while these are crucible moments
for leaders, they are also *tremendous* opportunities. When done right—by

getting facts and being visible, honest, calm, and optimistic—tremendous trust can be generated and team performance can soar.

KEY POINTS

1. In times of crisis—when there is great uncertainty—those organizations that proactively build trust up and down the chain of command will weather the storm much better than those that do not.

2. During a crisis, the behaviors of the leader have enormous influence.

3. The five key behaviors a leader must employ during a crisis are:
   - Get as many pertinent facts about the crisis as quickly as possible.
   - Be visible. Get in front of your people. Listen to their concerns. Schedule these events with some regularity.
   - Be honest. Tell them what they need to hear, not what they want to hear.
   - Be calm. Show a steady hand, a confident smile, and a calm disposition.
   - Be optimistic. Bring hope by creating a vision for life after the crisis passes.

CONCLUSION

What's the secret to leadership? How can you impact not only your subordinates' drive and passion for their jobs but also their overall health and well-being? How can you ensure your leadership is improving the bottom line, not harming it? How can you ensure your employees care about the work they're putting in and feel a sense of purpose in their day-to-day lives? How do you inspire people to go from point A to point B, particularly if they don't want to? How can an organization not only survive a crisis but also thrive while navigating through the storm? In the end, how can an organization not only accomplish its mission but also achieve organizational excellence?

After a journey of over thirty years in a variety of leadership jobs in the Navy, as well as immersing myself in research on the topic, I can tell you that the key is indeed as simple as the insights that I gained from Chief Tandy, Chief Smock, and cousin Steve all those years ago: take care of your people and they'll take care of you. Effective leadership is indeed not about command and control but about compassion and caring. That's it. A caring leader is a trusted leader, and a trusted leader is an effective leader.

How does a leader appropriately build a relationship with team members? What are some specific acts of caring that will help build trust up and down the chain of command? My experience, as well as extensive research, shows that the answer to those two questions can be found by employing the following six behaviors:

- Know your staff.
- Be visible.
- Always treat all staff with dignity and respect.
- Don't ignore good or poor performance.

- Be optimistic.
- Continuously learn the art of leadership.

These leadership behaviors are all practical and applicable. Who is able to employ them? Anyone. These behaviors are powerful, but they are not complex. Employing them takes energy, time, and discipline. As I mentioned in the introduction to this book, in order to optimize your effectiveness as a leader, all six of these behaviors need to be employed. You will not maximize trust and team performance if you employ one or two behaviors in isolation of the others.

A subordinate's trust in their leader is *the* most important factor in the success of any organization. Because of the enormous control that a leader wields over subordinates, leaders are intrinsically intimidating. Left untouched, this naturally generates more fear than trust, fear being the natural state of being. Whether a leader becomes more intimidating and generates more fear, or less intimidating and earns trust, will depend on the leader's behaviors. Many leaders are not aware of this vitally important concept. Here's the good news—you are not one of them! By proactively employing the behaviors described in this book, you can now reverse this natural state of affairs. These behaviors drive out fear, earn trust, build high-performing teams, and achieve organizational excellence.

At the end of the day, the only things we control 100 percent of the time are our behaviors. You now understand the incredible influence that your behaviors have on team performance. You'll now, correctly, start focusing more on what *you're* doing instead of on what *others* are doing. You'll spend more time being mindful of your vitally important role in *achieving* the result as opposed to spending time *watching* for the results.

Opportunities to show that you care and earn trust occur hundreds of times each day. They're in abundance and lay dormant in every interaction—at the water cooler, at a meeting, when passing in the hallway, in your text message, in a post, and during a social event, among a host of others. The great leaders appreciate that the key to unlocking the power in these interactions is in managing their behavior *during* the interaction. Great leaders know that employees emulate their behaviors, which creates a culture, a culture that determines team performance. The great leaders understand, respect, and fully embrace the staggering power of their behaviors. My hope is that I've inspired you to be one of those great leaders.

Be a great leader. Embrace the profound impact of your behaviors. Most importantly, enjoy the journey!

To learn more about how my company can help your team build trust up and down the chain of command and achieve organizational excellence, visit our website at www.broukerleadershipsolutions.com.

ACKNOWLEDGMENTS

I would first and foremost like to thank my wife, Kris, for your willingness to give up your criminal justice career very early in our marriage so that I could embark on this great Navy adventure. Because of your sacrifices and support, we were able to fully enjoy the incredible journey together. We moved thirteen times, lived in seven different states and three foreign countries, and visited many other states and countries. Without your support, I would not have completed a thirty-year Navy career, would not have had the opportunity to lead at the levels I did, and would not have the experience—and stories—that made this book possible. I thank you for your patience and understanding as I invested thousands of hours in the writing of this book. You helped me when I needed it and gave me the time to complete the project. On top of everything else, you spent countless hours editing and helping me to rewrite this manuscript. Thank you for unselfishly permitting me to pursue my professional passions—in the first thirty years of our marriage as a naval officer learning the art of leadership, and now as a professional speaker and author. I love you.

To my children, I thank you for your many sacrifices. My Navy career forced several moves, many times away from your friends. Like your mother, without your willingness to accept these sacrifices, my thirty-year Navy career, the opportunities to lead, and the experiences that made this book possible would not have happened. To Shayna, thank you for your encouragement to keep writing, especially when it was difficult to find the words. Thank you for doing an excellent job editing the manuscript. You have a beautiful gift for writing, and I encourage you to use it. You are an incredible mother, and both Kris and I love watching you grow in that role. To my son-in-law Joe, thank you for your honorable and unselfish service to our country, especially your two Army deployments into harm's way. I also thank you for your help in editing this manuscript and for being a wonderful father. To Jake, your service to our country as a Navy weapons systems officer on the F-18 Hornet is an inspiration to me each and every day you wear the cloth of the nation. You are at the tip of the spear, and my pride for your service is immeasurable. To Katherine, many thanks for your encouragement to write this book. Your amazing leadership on and off the volleyball court, before, during, and after your college volleyball career, continues to fuel my passion and inspire me to learn of the leadership phenomenon. To all our children, our grandchild Jonah, and future grandchildren, I hope this book will help you take full advantage of your many God-given talents and help you live your dreams.

To my parents, whose love and guidance are with me in everything I pursue, you continue to be the ultimate role models. To my dad, whose Navy stories were the impetus for my original interest in the Navy, thank you for the gift of humor and storytelling and passion for history, all of which were essential in the writing of this book. You have the gift of lifelong learning—you continue to read and learn to this day—as well as a passion for exercise. I am blessed that you gave me these gifts. To my mom, without ever saying it but through the way you always treat others, you gave me the gift of always treating everyone with dignity and respect. I don't *ever* recall you speaking ill of another person. This specific behavior is a core element in this book. You also gave me the gift of fully enjoying life, of taking advantage of every opportunity that comes. This helped inspire me to write this book; it was an opportunity I was compelled to pursue. To my cousin, CWO3 Steve Brouker, who helped me understand what true leadership looked like and helped me decide to join the Navy.

To my development editor, Lindsay Newton, many thanks for a thousand small things and maybe a couple dozen larger ones that rehabilitated my first and second drafts into prime form. You're an amazing editor and, more importantly, an absolute pleasure to work with. To my literary agent, Jeff Herman, many thanks for your wisdom and wise counsel. I'm very fortunate to have you in my corner. To Lori Ames and Caitlyn Sullivan with ThePRFreelancer, Inc., your outstanding help in getting the word out regarding this book is very much appreciated. My thanks go out to the team at Rowman & Littlefield—you've all been a pleasure to work with. To my friend, colleague, and shipmate Kurt

Houser, many thanks for your tremendous feedback on the innumerable questions that arose during the writing of this book. To Dr. Shiloh Beckerley, many thanks for your help with analyzing the data that emerged from the studies conducted by the Mental Health Advisory Team.

To all the men and women of the U.S. Navy and our sister services who served with me during my years on active duty and who continue to work with me now, and especially to my shipmates at U.S. Naval Hospital Bremerton during my command tour, I want to thank you for being the inspiration and foundation for this book. I also want to thank my colleagues at the Honor Foundation. You have given me the incredible opportunity to get to know Navy SEALs and the U.S. Special Operations community and help these amazing warriors transition from their military careers. Their heartfelt stories of caring, service, and sacrifice helped forge my conviction that these are the virtues upon which true effective leadership is built.

Finally, I want to thank the U.S. Navy leaders who gave me innumerable opportunities to lead others. I hope this book helps future generations of Navy leaders, and all leaders, learn the art of leadership.

APPENDIX: RECOMMENDED READING

Below are my top choices for books on leadership listed in alphabetical order by title. These books made the cut from the many that I've read primarily because each had a profound impact on me, as well as a unique role in molding me as a leader.

THE 7 HABITS OF HIGHLY EFFECTIVE PEOPLE (STEPHEN COVEY)

This is an absolutely exceptional and timeless book. I was introduced to it while attending my first leadership development seminar as a very young naval officer. Although many years have passed since then, I still recall how it changed my life. I've read it at least three times and still refer to it often. While all seven habits are important, and some are referenced in my book, the one that I believe helped me to be much more effective in all roles—husband, father, son, brother, friend, and, of course, naval officer—was "begin with the end in mind." In this chapter, Covey wisely asks the reader to envision attending their own funeral and imagining what the different speakers would say. It was a provocative exercise for me. This chapter helped me as I wrestled with the work-life balance conundrum.

EVERY TOWN IS A SPORTS TOWN (GEORGE BODENHEIMER)

This author tells the story of his amazing three-decade career at ESPN, where he literally advanced from mail clerk to president. His book identifies the leadership behaviors that were key to his tremendous success. Not surprisingly, they are know your staff, be visible, always treat others with respect, don't ignore good or bad performance, and be optimistic. It was refreshing to read of a highly accomplished sports executive who successfully used the exact behaviors described in my book to achieve organizational excellence.

FIRST, BREAK ALL THE RULES (MARCUS BUCKINGHAM AND CURT COFFMAN)

In this book, the authors, both employed at the Gallup Organization, successfully mine enormous amounts of data and present remarkable findings. Their research proves a vital link between employee opinions—dictated by the behaviors of the leader—and productivity, profit, customer satisfaction, and rate of turnover. I love this book because its solid research aligns exactly with what I experienced throughout my leadership journey.

GOOD TO GREAT (JIM COLLINS)

Using an enormous amount of data, Collins and his research team answer a vexing question: Why do some companies achieve sustained greatness while others remain only good? What I found intriguing about their conclusions is that all great companies were led by humble leaders. Reflecting back on the great leaders I have worked for, I also concluded that, indeed, all were humble. Interestingly, all the poor leaders I have worked for shared another trait: they were all arrogant. This book instilled in me the need to stay grounded, to never think too highly of myself, and to always treat others with respect. This lesson was an enormous help throughout my Navy career but especially during my tour as commanding officer.

HOW TO BECOME A CEO (JEFFREY FOX)

A quick read, this book provides seventy-five rules that offer practical advice on how to get ahead in the business world. I read this book while stationed in Rota, Spain, as the executive officer at the U.S. naval hospital. This book helped me to be a much more effective C-suite leader in Rota, a new role for me, and it helped prepare me for my command tour (which was my next tour at Naval Hospital Bremerton, Washington). It provides great examples of specific behaviors that impact culture. The simple rules described in this book are applicable for any leader at any level.

HOW TO WIN FRIENDS AND INFLUENCE PEOPLE (DALE CARNEGIE)

A truly timeless book, it was first published in 1936 and has sold over fifteen million copies worldwide, making it one of the best-selling books of all time. I read it in the late 1990s simply because I desperately wanted to influence a colleague. My relationship with this colleague was strained—the trust between us was minimal at best. Here's the story: I was accepted to give a presentation at a national conference, and my colleague was responsible for scheduling the speakers. Unfortunately, he scheduled me to be the *last* speaker on the *last* day of the conference. I was not happy, to say the least. I immediately assumed that, because of our strained relationship, he had done this to spite me. My first impulse was to call him and tell him what I thought of his schedule! Fortunately, I didn't. Instead, something gave me the wisdom to pick up this tremendous book. Using the techniques described, I was able to convince my colleague to move my talk to the first day. More importantly, our relationship improved significantly. This book gave me wisdom that I use to this day to check my temper and maintain civil discourse when provoked to anger.

LEADERSHIP: THE WARRIOR'S ART (CHRISTOPHER KOLENDA)

This book is an outstanding collection of historical and contemporary case studies written by experienced military professionals and top civilian leadership scholars. I love the book's theme that soldiers and organizations are capable of greatness if their leaders create mutual respect and trust. Leadership is about trust, and trust occurs when the leader cares for their soldiers. Indeed, leaders who took care of their soldiers led units that were the most combat effective, a concept that is eerily familiar to Chief Smock's quote referenced in my book. The book also delves into the immense power of leadership, using the term "special magic of leadership," which is unleashed when the leader touches the souls of others. How this power is unleashed has not changed over the millennia—it transcends time and context.

MASTERING CIVILITY (CHRISTINE PORATH)

This book is unique in that it includes solid scientific research to substantiate Dr. Porath's claim that, as a leader, it pays to be civil. While I personally learned the power of this behavior—always treat everyone with dignity and respect—through experience, it was refreshing to read numerous well-structured studies that all provided solid evidence of this concept. This book reinforced my convictions regarding the critical importance of a leader's behavior. I had the pleasure of having lunch with Dr. Porath at Georgetown University during one of my speaking trips to Washington, D.C. It was an absolute joy to meet someone who is as passionate about the topic of leadership as I am. Chapter 2 of her book gives some fascinating insight as to what fuels her passion.

PRIMAL LEADERSHIP (DANIEL GOLEMAN)

I read this book when it was first published in 2002, and it was my first exposure to the fascinating science of emotional intelligence (EI). It was captivating to learn that the leader's emotions are contagious: organizations led by energetic and enthusiastic leaders thrive; those led by pessimistic and disconnected leaders flounder. I've since been to a number of EI seminars and have become a strong advocate of the science. This book further reinforced my convictions regarding the critical importance of a leader's behavior.

SHACKLETON'S WAY (MARGOT MORRELL AND STEPHANIE CAPPARELL)

A tremendous leadership guide disguised as an adventure story. I've mentioned to countless audiences, including a Hollywood producer whom I met by chance on a train ride along the coast of Southern California, that the story depicted in this book would make a powerful movie—no changes needed, simply tell the story. While there are countless leadership lessons in this book, the most compelling was the power of optimism. You'll read how, despite being in a completely hopeless situation, Shackleton knew that the outcome of his team's life-and-death struggle hinged on his ability to maintain an air of optimism. I was fortunate to have come across this book during my command tour, which, like every leadership job, had its share of dark moments. This book was pivotal in reminding me of the importance of maintaining optimism in spite of difficult challenges.

THE ADMIRALS (WALTER BORNEMAN)

While there are innumerable leadership lessons throughout this masterpiece of research and storytelling about the four five-star admirals who helped the United States beat Japan during World War II, I was riveted by the stories and actions of Admiral Nimitz. Borneman does an excellent job highlighting how Nimitz used patience, tolerance, and understanding to successfully lead a diverse array of subordinates to victory in the Pacific.

THE CAPTAIN CLASS (SAM WALKER)

One of the most interesting books on leadership I've read. The author uses data to identify the greatest sports teams of all time and then explores what these outlier teams had in common. What did he find? All teams had one player who unified the team; they all had one great leader. Interestingly, most of these so-called glue players were players with average skill, not the team superstars. The crucial component of their job was interpersonal: they engaged with their teammates constantly with energy and enthusiasm, listening, observing, speaking to teammates as peers, counseling them on and off the field, motivating them, challenging them, protecting them, resolving disputes, enforcing standards, and inserting themselves into every meaningful moment. They tried to understand their teammates, to know their backgrounds. They created as many opportunities as possible to interact with each and every one of their teammates. In short, they led. The result was an amazing culture of trust that resulted in absolute peak performance. This book helped me appreciate that whether a sports team, a corporate team, or a nonprofit group, peak performance is driven by leaders who proactively build relationships with other team members, all of which earns trust.

THE GREAT WORKPLACE (JENNIFER ROBIN AND MICHAEL BURCHELL)

I came across this book shortly after completing my Navy career. This book impacted me in a profound way—for the first time, I found solid research that aligned exactly with what I had learned through experience. The authors, both Great Place to Work Institute insiders, show that what matters in corporate performance is the relationships that leaders build with employees. When leaders build strong employee-employer relationships, employees feel cared for and have a great workplace experience, a trusting culture is created, and team performance soars.

THE HOLY BIBLE

While I continue to struggle to carve out time to read and study this amazing book (the best-selling work of literature in the world), I've learned invaluable lessons on how to live life from its contents, and I studied it more when I faced significant work and life challenges. Specifically, during my tours at Navy Personnel Command and as commanding officer, each morning before work I'd read excerpts from both of John C. Maxwell's books, *Leadership Promises for Every Day: A Daily Devotional* and *One-Minute Prayers for Men*. Another book, *Leadership Proverbs: Wisdom for Today's Leaders*, by David Stevens and Bert Jones, which was graciously given to me as a gift from the family medicine residents from Naval Hospital Bremerton, I opened often during my transition from the Navy to the civilian sector. Readings from each of these books, and of course from the Holy Bible, kept me anchored during difficult times. There is a thread throughout the Bible that the true foundation of leadership is built upon relationships, love, service, and sacrifice. These virtues align well with the leadership behaviors described in my book.

THE LEADER'S BOOKSHELF (JAMES STAVRIDIS AND R. MANNING ANCELL)

This fascinating book was given to me by a friend and colleague (thanks, Captain Doug Stephens!). The authors surveyed more than two hundred active and retired four-star military officers regarding their reading habits and favorite books. The authors asked each for a list of titles that strongly influenced them as leaders. The book assembles their responses to identify the top fifty books. The authors list the concepts of leadership that emerged from the fifty books reviewed. Of the numerous leadership principles discussed, there were two common themes that ran through all fifty books. They were (1) the importance of optimism and (2) during times of crisis and uncertainty, the leader needs to remain calm, collected, and compassionate; when in the tempest, it is imperative that the leader remains respectful. Both behaviors align with what I experienced through my leadership journey and are supported by numerous studies. While I had already read many of the fifty books reviewed in this publication, this book is a rich source of many tremendous leadership books.

THE ONE MINUTE MANAGER (KENNETH BLANCHARD AND SPENCER JOHNSON)

First published in 1982, this classic is still changing the workplace and has global sales of over thirteen million. What I found refreshing about this book was the simplicity of the tools that keep employees motivated, happy, and performing at the highest level.

THE POWER OF POSITIVE THINKING
(NORMAN VINCENT PEALE)

Another timeless book, first published in 1952, it has sold over five million copies. I read it in the late 1990s, and it opened my eyes to the power of an optimistic attitude. More importantly, it gave me practical tips on how to maintain an air of optimism during life's challenges. In the 1990s, Kris and I had three young children and I was trying to balance my Navy career with family needs. They were challenging times, and this book helped me understand the importance of maintaining a positive attitude through it all.

NOTES

INTRODUCTION

1. A non-commissioned officer (NCO—colloquially, "non-com") is a military officer who has not earned a commission. Non-commissioned officers obtain their position of authority by promotion through the enlisted ranks. In contrast, commissioned officers hold higher ranks than NCOs, have more legal responsibilities, are paid more, and often have more non-military training, such as a university diploma. The non-commissioned officer corps is the "backbone" of the armed services, as they are the primary and most visible leaders for most military personnel. Senior NCOs are considered the primary link between enlisted personnel and commissioned officers in a military organization. Their advice and guidance are particularly important for junior officers, who begin their careers in a position of authority but generally lack practical experience.

2. Aristotle, *Politics*, 1314b18.

3. Plato, *Republic*, 342c, 345d, 347d.

4. Xenophon, *Cyropaedia* (*Education by Cyrus*), translated by Walter Miller (Cambridge, MA: Harvard University Press, Loeb Classical Library, 1914).

5. John Keegan, *Mask of Command* (New York: Penguin, 1987), 46.

6. Doris Kearns Goodwin, *Team of Rivals* (New York: Simon & Schuster, 2005).

7. Viktor Frankl, *Man's Search for Meaning* (Boston: Beacon Press, 1959), 80.

CHAPTER 1

1. Chief petty officer, more commonly known as "chief," is the seventh enlisted rank (E-7) in the United States Navy, just above petty officer first class (E-6) and below senior chief petty officer (E-8). The rank of chief petty officer is that of a senior non-commissioned officer. The primary role of the chief petty officer is bridg-

ing the gap between officers and enlisted personnel and overseeing the discipline, professional development, morale, training, welfare, and overall quality of life of all enlisted military personnel in the Navy. U.S. Navy chief petty officers are afforded more responsibility than any other enlisted rank in the world, and more than fifty chief petty officers have been awarded the Congressional Medal of Honor, the highest award that can be bestowed on an individual serving in the Armed Services of the United States.

2. Ensign is the most junior commissioned officer rank in the United States Navy.

3. The commanding officer (CO) is the officer in command of a military unit. The commanding officer has ultimate authority over the unit and is usually given wide latitude to run the unit as they see fit, within the bounds of military law.

4. Interestingly enough, as of the time of this book being published, I am the only pharmacy officer in the history of the Navy to be selected to command a family physician teaching hospital. During my command tour, Naval Hospital Bremerton was one of the Navy's five family physician teaching hospitals worldwide.

5. Active duty military members can be designated as being deployable, ready for operational assignment, or nondeployable based on their dental readiness. The Department of Defense requirement for all military personnel is 95 percent dental readiness. This requirement is in effect because previous studies have shown that higher dental readiness results in fewer mission-compromising incidents.

6. The assignment of an active duty member to a duty status for a specified time with certain medical limitations or restrictions concerning the duties the member may perform.

7. The Department of Defense (DoD) authorizes military treatment facilities to recover the cost of providing health-care services to covered DoD beneficiaries from third-party payers. The Third Party Collection Program is the military program established to accomplish this task.

8. The command climate survey (called the Defense Organization Climate Survey) is an employee engagement tool used by the Department of Defense to assess the leadership effectiveness of the commanding officer. It is an anonymous survey given to all members of the unit (command) at least annually and assesses the members' trust in their leaders. Among topics evaluated are perceptions of favoritism, organizational effectiveness, equal opportunity, equal employment opportunity, fair treatment, diversity management, organizational processes, intention to stay in the Navy, help-seeking behaviors, exhaustion or burnout, demeaning behaviors, hazing, and sexual assault prevention and response.

9. The Integrated Disability Evaluation System (IDES) is used to determine if service members coping with wounds that may prevent them from performing their duties are able to continue serving. The IDES is a joint process established by the

Department of Veterans Affairs and the Department of Defense that includes a single set of disability medical examinations and disability ratings for use by both departments.

10. Force protection (FP) consists of preventive measures taken by commands to mitigate hostile actions against Department of Defense personnel (including family members), resources, facilities, and critical information.

11. Family physicians complete an undergraduate degree, medical school, and three more years of specialized medical residency training in family medicine at an accredited family physician teaching hospital. At the time of my command tour, Naval Hospital Bremerton was one of the Navy's five family physician teaching hospitals worldwide.

12. In order to become board certified, family physicians must complete a residency in family medicine, possess a full and unrestricted medical license, and take a written cognitive examination.

13. Gallup, "State of the American Workplace, 2017," www.gallup.com/work place/238085/state-american-workplace-report-2017.aspx.

14. Jeff Schwartz and Ardie Van Berkel, "The Overwhelmed Employee— Simplify the Work Environment," *Deloitte Insights*, March 7, 2014, 97–102.

CHAPTER 2

1. The Bureau of Naval Personnel in the United States Department of the Navy is similar to the human resources department of a corporation. The bureau provides administrative leadership and policy planning for the Office of the Chief of Naval Operations and the U.S. Navy at large.

2. A fitness report is an evaluation used by the United States Navy and United States Marine Corps to periodically assess an officer's performance. These evaluations are the most important determinants of whether an officer will be promoted to the next rank.

3. Mental Health Advisory Team, Mental Health Advisory Team (MHAT-VI) Report, 2009. Accessed February 12, 2020. www.armymedicine.army.mil/reports/mhat/mhat_vi/mhat-vi.cfm.

4. A platoon is a military unit typically consisting of approximately twenty to forty soldiers. A platoon leader is the officer in command of a platoon. A platoon is typically the smallest military unit led by a commissioned officer.

5. Mental Health Advisory Team, Mental Health Advisory Team (MHAT-VI) Report, 2009. Accessed February 12, 2020.

6. Christopher Kolenda, *Leadership: The Warrior's Art* (Carlisle, PA: Army War College Foundation Press, 2001), 41.

7. Michael Bush, *A Great Place to Work for All* (Oakland, CA: Berrett-Koehler, 2018), 26.

8. Gallup, "State of the American Workplace, 2017." Accessed February 12, 2020.

9. Bradley Owens and David Hekman, "How Does Leader Humility Influence Team Performance? Exploring the Mechanisms of Contagion and Collective Promotion Focus," *Academy of Management Journal*, April 30, 2015, https://journals.aom.org/doi/10.5465/amj.2013.0660.

CHAPTER 3

1. Robert Klemko, "Success of Robert Griffin III Boosts Shanahans' Stock," *USA Today*, December 28, 2012.

2. The base commander is the officer assigned to command a military base. In the United States Armed Forces, a base commander is generally an O-6 grade officer, which means colonel (Army, Air Force, Marines) or captain (Navy, Coast Guard).

3. Command sergeant major, or CSM, is the most senior enlisted member within an Army unit and is the senior enlisted advisor to the base commander. They are responsible for much of the direction and performance of the enlisted personnel within their military unit, maintaining good order and discipline of enlisted troops.

4. An Individual Augmentee is a U.S. military member attached to a unit (battalion or company) as a temporary duty assignment. Individual Augmentees can be used to fill shortages or when an individual with specialized knowledge or skill sets is required. As a result, Individual Augmentees can include members from an entirely different branch of service. The system was used extensively in both the Iraq War and the Afghanistan War and is still used in the latter conflict as of time of publication. By early 2007, there were an average of approximately twelve thousand Navy personnel filling Army jobs in the United States, Iraq, Afghanistan, Cuba, and the Horn of Africa at any one time. Approximately 15 percent of my active duty staff at Naval Hospital Bremerton were deployed as Individual Augmentees at any one time during my three years in command.

5. Family reintegration can be a turbulent time for the family, as members must re-form into a functioning system. One of the greatest challenges for these families is renegotiating family roles as the service member encounters the often-unexpected difficulty of fitting into a home routine that has likely changed a great deal since their departure. Typically, the at-home parent and children assume new responsibilities such that when the service member returns, there may be expectations among family members that things will return to how they were prior to deployment or, conversely, that the structure that emerged during deployment will remain.

6. Mortuary Affairs is a service within the United States Army Quartermaster Corps tasked with the retrieval, identification, transportation, and burial of deceased American and American-allied military personnel. Until 1991, it was known as the Graves Registration Service. The Graves Registration Service was created several months after the United States entered World War I.

7. Michael Sledge, *Soldier Dead: How We Recover, Identify, Bury, and Honor Our Military Fallen* (New York: Columbia University Press, 2007).

8. The U.S. Navy has two hospital ships. The USNS *Mercy*, homeported in San Diego, and the USNS *Comfort*, homeported in Norfolk, Virginia.

9. Following Operation Unified Endeavour, the United States' response to the 2004 Indian Ocean earthquake and tsunami, the United States Navy saw the opportunity to build on the goodwill created by this operation and conceived an annual deployment to the region. Before the U.S. response to the tsunami, the approval rating for the United States in Indonesia was 15 percent. After the U.S. response to the tsunami, the approval rating more than doubled to 38 percent. The aim of the annual deployment, titled Pacific Partnership, is to improve the interoperability of the region's military forces, governments, and humanitarian organizations during disaster relief operations, while providing humanitarian, medical, dental, and engineering assistance to nations of the Pacific and strengthening relationships and security ties between the nations. The first such deployment was conducted in 2006, based aboard the hospital ship USNS *Mercy*, and included partner nations such as Australia and nongovernmental organizations. Pacific Partnership deployments have visited the Philippines, Cambodia, Vietnam, Bangladesh, Indonesia, West Timor, and East Timor.

10. An HM3 is an enlisted sailor, a petty officer third class who is a hospital corpsman (HM).

11. According to Islamic law ("shariah"), the body should be buried as soon as possible after the time of death. Ideally, the funeral will take place before the next sunset or within twenty-four hours.

12. One of the many tactics described to help win in counterinsurgency warfare involves the use of public diplomacy through military means. Counterinsurgency is effective when it is integrated into a comprehensive strategy employing all instruments of national power, including public diplomacy. The goal is to render the enemy insurgents ineffective and noninfluential by having strong and secure relations with the population of the host nation. Honoring shariah law and Islam in regard to burial ceremonies is a perfect example of public diplomacy supporting counterinsurgency warfare.

13. A civil action program, also known as a civic action project, is a type of operation designed to assist an area by using the capabilities and resources of a military force or civilian organization to conduct long-term programs or short-term projects.

This type of operation includes a dental civic action program, engineering civic action program, medical civic action program, and veterinarian civic action program. Entities of foreign nations usually conduct these operations at the invitation of a host nation.

14. GlobalSecurity.org, "Evolution of the Chemical Warfare Program," Iraq Survey Group Final Report, September 30, 2004, www.globalsecurity.org/wmd/library/report/2004/isg-final-report/.

15. "Anniversary of Baath Party Chemical Attack on Innocent People in Halabja / Saddam Genocide in Iraqi Kurdistan," *Taghrib News*, March 1, 2009, www.taghribnews.com/fa/news/409468.

16. Foroutan Abbas, *Medical Experiences of Iraq's Chemical Warfare* (Tehran: Baqiya-tallah University Medical Science, 2003).

17. Commander Deeter was the senior POMI (plans, operations, and medical intelligence) officer. His primary responsibility was to ensure that the *Comfort* had the right mix of staff to accomplish its mission of receiving and treating casualties. As such, his team decided who would deploy and who would stay behind. There were a number of factors that made Commander Deeter's job especially challenging. Three prominent factors were (1) Saddam's invasion came as a complete surprise, (2) this was *Comfort*'s first deployment, and (3) this was the United States' first mass mobilization of forces in a generation (nearly twenty years).

18. This story gives the reader an idea of how dynamic the situation was regarding who was deploying and who was staying. I've often wondered what would have happened if I had not decided to talk with Commander Deeter that morning, or, when leaving his office, if I had decided to take the stairs as opposed to choosing the slow elevator. It's likely that the buses, which left shortly after this interaction, would have departed without me.

19. David Moore, "Americans Believe U.S. Participation in Gulf War a Decade Ago Worthwhile," Gallup News Service, February 26, 2001.

20. SCUD is the name of a series of tactical ballistic missiles developed by the Soviet Union during the Cold War. These missiles were exported widely to both Second and Third World countries, including Iraq. Saddam used this weapon extensively in the Persian Gulf War.

21. When needed, military members were issued a pair of glasses for "battlefield" scenarios. The glasses consisted of a rubberized frame with an adjustable rubber strap. The strap held the lenses close to the face to make it easier to quickly don the MOPP gear and gas mask.

22. Intercepts of Iraqi military communications indicated that Saddam had authorized frontline commanders to use chemical weapons at their discretion as soon as coalition forces began their ground war. A number of factors precluded this option. The remarkable speed of the coalition advance, combined with the effectiveness of

the strategic bombing campaign in disrupting Iraq's military command-and-control system, made it difficult for Iraqi commanders to select battlefield targets for chemical attacks. Furthermore, the prevailing winds (which for six months had blown from the northwest out of Iraq) shifted at the beginning of the ground war to the southeast, toward the Iraqi lines (Jonathan Tucker, "Evidence Iraq Used Chemical Weapons during the 1991 Persian Gulf War," *The Nonproliferation Review* [Spring–Summer 1997]).

23. Interestingly, this was the last major war in which the written letter was the primary mode of communication between faraway warriors and their loved ones back home; we were communicating with our loved ones the same way soldiers under General Washington did during the American Revolution two hundred years earlier. The first major commercial internet service providers—American Online, Prodigy, and CompuServe—became available in 1995, four years after the Persian Gulf War ended. Regarding phone calls, no one on the *Comfort*, nor any loved ones back home, had cell phones. Cell phones were not yet generally available. In 1993, IBM Simon was introduced, which is largely considered to be the world's first smartphone. In 1992, there were only 7 million cell phone subscribers in the United States compared to 265 million at the time of writing. About every four to five weeks, the *Comfort* would pull into Bahrain, Abu Dhabi, or Dubai, and the crew would have a chance to get off the ship to explore the area and make phone calls to the United States from either pay phones or hotel rooms. The cost of these phone calls could run into the hundreds of dollars.

24. Department of Defense planners were anticipating twenty thousand casualties, including seven thousand killed in action in the first five days of combat during the ground offensive. The *Comfort* was on station off the coast of Kuwait during the ground offensive to receive and treat the thousands of expected casualties. Miraculously, only 154 U.S. service members were killed in battle. The *Comfort* did not receive or treat *any* casualties. While we were extremely joyful that we had no patients to treat, it was a surreal ending to a fascinating eight-month experience. See Richard Swain, *Lucky War: Third Army in Desert Storm* (Ft. Leavenworth, KS: U.S. Army Command and General Staff College Press, 1994).

CHAPTER 4

1. Military creases are formed by pressing two vertical creases in the front of the shirt, from the shoulder seam through the center of each pocket to the bottom of the shirt, and three evenly spaced vertical creases in the back of the shirt.

2. The executive officer, also known as XO, is the second-in-command of a military unit, reporting to the commanding officer. The XO is typically responsible

for the management of day-to-day activities, freeing the commanding officer to concentrate on strategy and planning the unit's next move.

3. A command master chief petty officer, better known as a command master chief or CMC, is the most senior enlisted sailor in a United States Navy unit. The CMC is an important resource for the commanding officer and is often called on to gauge morale and battle readiness.

4. The comptroller is the chief financial officer of a Navy command.

5. Madrid is about four hundred miles north of Naval Hospital Rota. The vast majority of staff reporting to Naval Station Rota, including, of course, the U.S. Naval Hospital, arrived via Madrid and cleared customs at the Madrid airport. After clearing customs, they would then board a connecting flight to a city in southern Spain.

6. American military commissaries sell groceries and household goods to active duty, Guard, Reserve, and retired members of all seven uniformed services of the United States and eligible members of their families.

7. "Chief's mess" is a slang term to describe the group of enlisted Navy noncommissioned officers including the paygrade of E-7 (chief petty officer), E-8 (senior chief petty officer), and E-9 (master chief petty officer). Collectively they are the technical experts and leaders who implement good order and discipline. They routinely enforce the commanding officer's policies and procedures that significantly contribute to the ship's mission, combat readiness, and command climate.

8. Members of the military are eligible to retire if they serve on active duty in the U.S. Army, Navy, Air Force, or Marine Corps for twenty years.

9. Mark Murphy, "Neuroscience Explains Why You Need to Write Down Your Goals If You Actually Want to Achieve Them," *Forbes*, April 15, 2018, www.forbes .com/sites/markmurphy/2018/04/15/neuroscience-explains-why-you-need-to -write-down-your-goals-if-you-actually-want-to-achieve-them/#275ce00c7905.

10. Selen Turkay, "Setting Goals: Who, Why, How," Harvard Office of the Vice Provost for Advances in Learning, 2014, https://vpal.harvard.edu/publications/year/ 2014.

11. Edwin Locke and Gary Latham, "Building a Practically Useful Theory of Goal Setting and Task Motivation: A 35-Year Odyssey," *American Psychologist* 57 (2002): 705–17.

12. Gary Latham and Edwin Locke, "Goal Setting: A Motivational Technique That Works," *Organizational Dynamics* 8, no. 2 (1979): 68–80.

13. At that time, Naval Hospital Bremerton had 16 percent of their active duty staff members deployed, mostly to Afghanistan and Iraq. Many positions remained unfilled for the duration of the member's deployment, some of which were up to fifteen months.

CHAPTER 5

1. This government budget crisis was ultimately resolved, and the federal government did not shut down. For clarity, a government shutdown happens when government offices can no longer remain open due to lack of funding, which usually occurs when there is a delay in the approval of the federal budget by Congress for the upcoming fiscal year.

2. U.S. Naval Hospital Bremerton was a stand-alone command. It comprised an expansive complex of buildings enclosed by a security fence. My XO, Ken Iverson, had not yet reported onboard the command. When he did, our routine was to exercise together at noon.

3. Buildings on U.S. Military bases for quartering enlisted personnel.

4. In the U.S. Navy, the Command Ashore insignia is a gold badge worn on the breast of one's uniform that recognizes the responsibilities and importance of command ashore and major program management. It is commonly referred to as a command pin.

CHAPTER 6

1. Christine Porath, *Mastering Civility* (New York: Hachette, 2016), 32.

2. The Joint Commission is an organization that accredits more than 22,000 military and civilian health-care programs.

3. The Navy Medical Inspector General Program is tasked with inspecting, investigating, or inquiring into matters of importance to the Medical Department of the Navy.

4. "Junior officer," "company officer," or "company grade officer" refers to the lowest operational commissioned officer category of ranks in a military organization, ranking above non-commissioned officers and below senior officers.

5. While we never found out the specifics regarding how the leg remained lost in the corner of a freezer for over five years, we conducted a thorough root cause analysis. We learned some information regarding the incident, including identifying and contacting the patient. We instituted procedures that improved the process and I divulged all of this to the inspectors. We passed both inspections.

6. Paul Zak, "The Neuroscience of Trust," *Harvard Business Review* (January–February 2017).

7. Paul Zak, *Trust Factor* (New York: American Management Association, 2017), 20, 21, 119.

8. R. M. Sapolsky, *Why Zebras Don't Have Ulcers*, 3rd ed. (New York: Owl Books/Henry Holt, 2004).

9. Christine Porath, *Mastering Civility* (New York: Hachette, 2016), 15.

10. S. Lim, L. M. C ortina, and V. J. Magley, "Personal and Workgroup Incivility: Impact on Work and Health Outcomes," *Journal of Applied Psychology* 93, no. 1 (2008): 95–107.

11. A. Shirom et al., "Work-Based Predictors of Mortality: A 20-Year Follow-Up of Healthy Employees," *Health Psychology* 30, no. 3 (2011): 268–75.

12. M. Ferguson, "You Cannot Leave It at the Office: Spillover and Crossover of Coworker Incivility," *Journal of Organizational Behavior* 33, no 4 (2011): 571–88.

13. Christine Porath, *Mastering Civility* (New York: Hachette, 2016), 17.

14. Albert Risken et al., "The Impact of Rudeness on Medical Team Performance: A Randomized Trial," *Pediatrics* 136 (2015): 487–95.

15. Necrotizing enterocolitis, or NEC, is the most common and serious intestinal disease among premature babies.

16. Randall Engle and Michael Kane, "Executive Attention, Working Memory Capacity, and a Two-Factor Theory of Cognitive Control," *The Psychology of Learning and Motivation* 44 (2004): 145–99.

17. Shore-based military installations are staffed by both active duty military members and government service (GS) civilian employees. Active duty members typically work well in excess of traditional forty-hour work weeks. Therefore, when possible, many shore-based military installations grant active duty members an additional vacation day during three-day holidays, for a total of four consecutive free vacation days. GS civilian employees are not granted this additional free vacation day.

18. The officer of the day (OOD) is a detail rotated each day among the military unit's commissioned and non-commissioned officers. The OOD oversees security, guard, and law enforcement considerations and is responsible for carrying out the missions of the unit during off-duty hours.

CHAPTER 7

1. Jean-Pierre Brun and Ninon Dugas, "An Analysis of Employee Recognition: Perspectives on Human Resources Practices," *The International Journal of Human Resource Management* 19, no. 4 (2008): 716–30.

2. Carolyn Wiley, "What Motivates Employees According to Over 40 Years of Motivation Surveys," *International Journal of Manpower* 18 (1997): 263–80.

3. Haiyan Zhang, "How Do I Recognize Thee, Let Me Count the Ways," Thought Leadership Whitepaper, IBM Smarter Workforce Institute, 2015.

4. Stephen Covey, *The 7 Habits of Highly Effective People* (New York: Free Press, 1989).

5. Colonoscopy is a test that allows a doctor to look at the inner lining of the large intestine (rectum and colon) and is principally used to diagnose colon cancer.

CHAPTER 8

1. Margot Morrell and Stephanie Capparell, *Shackleton's Way* (New York: Penguin, 2001).

2. Hỏa Lò Prison was used by the French colonists in Vietnam for political prisoners and later by North Vietnam for U.S. prisoners of war during the Vietnam War. During this later period, it was known to American POWs as the Hanoi Hilton. The prison was demolished in the 1990s, although the gatehouse remains as a museum.

3. Jim Collins, *Good to Great* (New York: HarperCollins, 2001).

4. Jim Collins, *Good to Great* (New York: HarperCollins, 2001).

5. Jim Collins, *Good to Great* (New York: HarperCollins, 2001).

6. Alan Axelrod, *Winston Churchill, CEO* (New York: Sterling, 2009).

7. Stephen Covey, *The 7 Habits of Highly Effective People* (New York: Free Press, 1989), 81.

8. Rick Atkinson, *An Army at Dawn* (New York: Henry Holt, 2002), 60–61.

9. Rick Atkinson, *An Army at Dawn* (New York: Henry Holt, 2002), 61.

10. Stephanie Grassullo, "A CEO's Letter to Employees Urges Them to Put Their Kids First," *The Bump*, December 5, 2018, www.thebump.com/news/ceo-charity-delmo-open-letter-parent-employees.

11. Michelle Arthur, "Share Price Reactions to Work-Family Human Resource Decisions: An Institutional Perspective," *Academy of Management Journal* 46 (2003): 497–505.

12. Edward Shepard et al., "Flexible Work Hours and Productivity: Some Evidence from the Pharmaceutical Industry," *Industrial Relations* 35, no. 1 (1996): 123–39.

13. Samuel Aryee et al., "Family-Responsive Variables and Retention-Relevant Outcomes among Employed Parents," *Human Relations* 51, no. 1 (1998): 73–87.

14. Jill Perry-Smith and Terry Blum, "Work-Life Human Resource Bundles and Perceived Organizational Performance," *Academy of Management Journal* 43, no. 6 (2000): 1107–17.

15. Stella Anderson et al., "Formal Organizational Initiatives and Informal Workplace Practices: Links to Work-Life Conflict and Job-Related Outcomes, Initiatives and Informal Workplace Practices: Links to Work-Life Conflict and Job-Related Outcomes," *Journal of Management* 28, no. 6 (2002): 787–810.

16. In the U.S. Armed Forces, nonjudicial punishment (NJP) is a form of military justice authorized by Article 15 of the Uniform Code of Military Justice. In the Navy, these NJP proceedings are referred to as Captain's Masts. NJP permits commanders to administratively discipline troops without a court-martial. It's a leadership tool providing military commanders a prompt and essential means of maintaining good order and discipline. Punishment can range from reprimand to reduction in rank, correctional custody, loss of pay, extra duty, and/or restrictions.

17. Arthur Kramer et al., "Ageing, Fitness and Neurocognitive Function," *Nature* 400 (1999): 418–19.

18. Thorleif Etgen et al., "Physical Activity and Incident Cognitive Impairment in Elderly Persons," *Archives of Internal Medicine* 170, no. 2 (2010): 186–93.

19. Maria Aberg et al., "Cardiovascular Fitness Is Associated with Cognition in Young Adulthood," The Salk Institute for Biological Studies, San Diego, CA, November 30, 2009, https://doi.org/10.1073/pnas.0905307106.

20. Christie Aschwanden et al., "Studies Show the Long-Term, Positive Effects of Fitness on Cognitive Abilities, Physical Activity May Be Important Not Just in Childhood But Also in Later Years," *The Washington Post Health & Science*, December 9, 2013.

21. Pew Research Center, *Religion's Relationship to Happiness, Civic Engagement and Health around the World*, January 31, 2019.

22. Karel Mentor et al., *Fundamentals of Naval Leadership* (Annapolis, MD: Naval Institute Press, 1984).

CHAPTER 9

1. Douglas Riddle, "Executive Integration Equipping Transitioning Leaders for Success," Center for Creative Leadership White Paper, 2016, www.ccl.org/wp-content/uploads/2015/04/ExecutiveIntegration.pdf.

2. Michael Beer et al., "Why Leadership Training Fails—and What to Do about It," *Harvard Business Review* online, October 2016, https://hbr.org/2016/10/why-leadership-training-fails-and-what-to-do-about-it.

CHAPTER 10

1. Kim Scott, "Workplaces Attuned to the Humanity of the Workers," *Wall Street Journal*, March 28–29, 2020.

2. Operation Uphold Democracy was a U.S.-led military intervention designed

to remove the military regime installed by the 1991 Haitian coup d'état that overthrew the elected president Jean-Bertrand Aristide.

3. Sheryl Sandberg, *Lean In: Women, Work, and the Will to Lead* (New York: Alfred A. Knopf, 2013), 91.

BIBLIOGRAPHY

Abbas Foroutan, Syed. *Medical Experiences of Iraq's Chemical Warfare*. Tehran: Baqiya-tallah University Medical Science, 2003.

Aberg, Maria, et al. "Cardiovascular Fitness Is Associated with Cognition in Young Adulthood." The Salk Institute for Biological Studies, San Diego, CA, November 30, 2009. https://doi.org/10.1073/pnas.0905307106.

Anderson, Stella, et al. "Formal Organizational Initiatives and Informal Workplace Practices: Links to Work-Life Conflict and Job-Related Outcomes." *Journal of Management* 28, no. 6 (2002): 787–810.

"Anniversary of Baath Party Chemical Attack on Innocent People in Halabja / Sad-dam Genocide in Iraqi Kurdistan." *Taghrib News*, March 1, 2009. www.taghrib news.com/fa/news/409468.

Aristotle. *Politics*.

Arthur, Michelle. "Share Price Reactions to Work-Family Human Resource Deci-sions: An Institutional Perspective." *Academy of Management Journal* 46 (2003): 497–505.

Aryee, Samuel, et al. "Family-Responsive Variables and Retention-Relevant Out-comes among Employed Parents." *Human Relations* 51, no. 1 (1998): 73–87.

Aschwanden, Christie, et al. "Studies Show the Long-Term, Positive Effects of Fit-ness on Cognitive Abilities, Physical Activity May Be Important Not Just in Child-hood But Also in Later Years." *The Washington Post Health & Science*, December 9, 2013.

Atkinson, Rick. *An Army at Dawn*. New York: Henry Holt and Company, 2002.

Axelrod, Alan. *Winston Churchill, CEO*. New York: Sterling, 2009.

Beer, Michael, et al. "Why Leadership Training Fails—and What to Do About It."

Harvard Business Review online, October 2016. https://hbr.org/2016/10/why -leadership-training-fails-and-what-to-do-about-it.

Blanchard, Ken, and Spencer Johnson. *The One Minute Manager*. New York: William Morrow, 1982.

Bodenheimer, George. *Every Town Is a Sports Town*. New York: Hachette, 2015.

Borneman, Walter. *The Admirals*. New York: Back Bay Books, 2012.

Bossidy, Larry, and Ram Charan. *Execution*. New York: Crown Business, 2002.

Bradberry, Travis, and Jean Greaves. *Emotional Intelligence 2.0*. San Diego, CA: TalentSmart, 2009.

Brun, Jean-Pierre, and Ninon Dugas. "An Analysis of Employee Recognition: Perspectives on Human Resources Practices." *The International Journal of Human Resource Management* 19, no. 4 (2008): 716–30.

Buckingham, Marcus, and Curt Coffman. *First, Break All the Rules*. New York: Simon & Schuster, 1999.

Burchell, Michael, and Jennifer Robin. *The Great Workplace*. New York: Jossey-Bass, 2011.

Bush, Michael. *A Great Place to Work for All*. Oakland, CA: Berrett-Koehler, 2018.

Calipari, John. *Players First*. New York: Penguin, 2014.

Campbell, Donovan. *Joker One*. New York: Random House, 2009.

Carnegie, Dale. *How to Win Friends and Influence People*. New York: Simon & Schuster, 1936.

Collins, Jim. *Good to Great*. New York: HarperCollins, 2001.

Covey, Stephen. *The 7 Habits of Highly Effective People*. New York: Free Press, 1989.

Engle, Randall, and Michael Kane. "Executive Attention, Working Memory Capacity, and a Two-Factor Theory of Cognitive Control." *The Psychology of Learning and Motivation* 44 (2004): 145–99.

Etgen, Thorleif, et al. "Physical Activity and Incident Cognitive Impairment in Elderly Persons." *Archives of Internal Medicine* 170, no. 2 (2010): 186–93.

Ferguson, M. "You Cannot Leave It at the Office: Spillover and Crossover of Coworker Incivility." *Journal of Organizational Behavior* 33, no 4 (2011): 571–88.

Fox, Jeffrey. *How to Become a CEO*. New York: Hyperion, 1998.

Frankl, Viktor. *Man's Search for Meaning*. Boston: Beacon Press, 1959.

Gallup. "State of the American Workplace, 2017." www.gallup.com/workplace/ 238085/state-american-workplace-report-2017.aspx.

Gladwell, Malcolm. *The Tipping Point*. New York: Little Brown, 2000.

GlobalSecurity.org. "Evolution of the Chemical Warfare Program." Iraq Survey Group Final Report, September 30, 2004. www.globalsecurity.org/wmd/library/ report/2004/isg-final-report/.

Goleman, Daniel, and Richard Boyatzis. *Primal Leadership*. Boston, MA: Harvard Business School, 2002.

Grassullo, Stephanie. "A CEO's Letter to Employees Urges Them to Put Their Kids First." *The Bump*, December 5, 2018. www.thebump.com/news/ceo-charity-de lmo-open-letter-parent-employees.

Harari, Oren. *The Leadership Secrets of Colin Powell*. New York: McGraw-Hill, 2002.

The Holy Bible, King James Version. New York: Random House, 1991.

Kearns Goodwin, Doris. *Leadership in Turbulent Times*. New York: Simon & Schuster, 2018.

Kearns Goodwin, Doris. *Team of Rivals: The Political Genius of Abraham Lincoln*. New York: Simon & Schuster, 2005.

Keegan, John. *The Mask of Command*. New York: Penguin, 1987.

Kolenda, Christopher. *Leadership: The Warrior's Art*. Carlisle, PA: The Army War College Foundation Press, 2001.

Kramer, Arthur, et al. "Ageing, Fitness and Neurocognitive Function." *Nature* 400 (1999): 418–19.

Latham, Gary, and Edwin Locke. "Goal Setting: A Motivational Technique That Works." *Organizational Dynamics* 8, no. 2 (1979): 68–80.

Laver, Harry, and Jeffrey Matthews. *The Art of Command*. Lexington, KY: The University Press of Kentucky, 2008.

Lencioni, Patrick. *The Advantage*. San Francisco, CA: Jossey-Bass, 2012.

Lim, S., L. M. Cortina, and V. J. Magley. "Personal and Workgroup Incivility: Impact on Work and Health Outcomes." *Journal of Applied Psychology* 93, no. 1 (2008): 95–107.

Locke, Edwin, and Gary Latham. "Building a Practically Useful Theory of Goal Setting and Task Motivation: A 35-Year Odyssey." *American Psychologist* 57 (2002): 705–17.

Marshall, Joey. "Are Religious People Happier, Healthier? Our New Global Study Explores This Question." Pew Research Center, Fact Tank, January 31, 2019. www.pewresearch.org/fact-tank/2019/01/31/are-religious-people-happier-healthier-our-new-global-study-explores-this-question/.

Maxwell, John C. *The 21 Irrefutable Laws of Leadership*. Nashville, TN: Thomas Nelson, 1998.

Mental Health Advisory Team (MHAT) (2009). Mental Health Advisory Team (MHAT-VI) report. From www.armymedicine.army.mil/reports/mhat/mhat_vi/mhat-vi.cfm.

Mentor, Karel, et al. *Fundamentals of Naval Leadership*. Annapolis, MD: Naval Institute Press, 1984.

Metcalf, C. W., and Roma Felible. *Lighten Up*. Reading, MA: Addison-Wesley, 1992.

Moore, David. "Americans Believe U.S. Participation in Gulf War a Decade Ago Worthwhile." Gallup News Service, February 26, 2001.

Morrell, Margot, and Stephanie Capparell. *Shackleton's Way*. New York: Penguin, 2001.

Murphy, Mark. "Neuroscience Explains Why You Need to Write Down Your Goals If You Actually Want to Achieve Them." *Forbes*, April 15, 2018. www.forbes .com/sites/markmurphy/2018/04/15/neuroscience-explains-why-you-need-to -write-down-your-goals-if-you-actually-want-to-achieve-them/#275ce00c7905.

Newmark, Jonathan. "The Birth of Nerve Agent Warfare: Lessons from Syed Abbas Foroutan." *Neurology* 62, no. 9 (May 11, 2004). https://n.neurology.org/content/ 62/9/1590.short.

Owens, Bradley, and David Hekman. "How Does Leader Humility Influence Team Performance? Exploring the Mechanisms of Contagion and Collective Promotion Focus." *Academy of Management Journal*, April 30, 2015. https://journals.aom.org/ doi/10.5465/amj.2013.0660.

Peale, Norman Vincent. *The Power of Positive Thinking*. New York: Prentice-Hall, 1952.

Perry-Smith, Jill, and Terry Blum. "Work-Life Human Resource Bundles and Perceived Organizational Performance." *Academy of Management Journal* 43, no. 6 (2000): 1107–17.

Phillips, Donald. *Lincoln on Leadership*. New York: Warner, 1992.

Plato, *Republic*.

Porath, Christine. *Mastering Civility*. New York: Hachette, 2016.

Riddle, Douglas. "Executive Integration Equipping Transitioning Leaders for Success." Center for Creative Leadership White Paper, 2016. www.ccl.org/wp-con tent/uploads/2015/04/ExecutiveIntegration.pdf.

Risken, Albert, et al. "The Impact of Rudeness on Medical Team Performance: A Randomized Trial." *Pediatrics* 136 (2015): 487–95.

Sandberg, Sheryl. *Lean In: Women, Work, and the Will to Lead*. New York: Alfred A. Knopf, 2013.

Sapolsky, R. M. *Why Zebras Don't Have Ulcers*. 3rd ed. New York: Owl Books/ Henry Holt, 2004.

Schwartz, Jeff, and Ardie Van Berkel. "The Overwhelmed Employee—Simplify the Work Environment." Deloitte Insights, March 7, 2014. www2.deloitte.com/us/ en/insights/focus/human-capital-trends/2014/hc-trends-2014-overwhelmed-em ployee.html.

Scott, Kim. "Workplaces Attuned to the Humanity of the Workers." *Wall Street Journal*, March 28–29, 2020.

Shirom, A., et al. "Work-Based Predictors of Mortality: A 20-Year Follow-Up of Healthy Employees." *Health Psychology* 30, no. 3 (2011): 268–75.

Sessa, Valerie, and Jodi Taylor. *Executive Selection*. San Francisco, CA: Jossey-Bass, 2000.

Shepard, Edward, et al. "Flexible Work Hours and Productivity: Some Evidence from the Pharmaceutical Industry." *Industrial Relations* 35, no. 1 (1996): 123–39.

Sledge, Michael. *Soldier Dead: How We Recover, Identify, Bury, and Honor Our Military Fallen.* New York: Columbia University Press, 2007.

Spiegelman, Paul, and Britt Berrett. *Patients Come Second.* New York: Greenleaf, 2013.

Stavridis, James, and R. Manning Ancell. *The Leader's Bookshelf.* Annapolis, MD: Naval Institute Press, 2017.

Strock, James. *Theodore Roosevelt on Leadership.* Roseville, CA: Prima, 2001.

Swain, Richard. *Lucky War: Third Army in Desert Storm.* Ft. Leavenworth, KS: U.S. Army Command and General Staff College Press, 1994.

Tucker, Jonathan. "Evidence Iraq Used Chemical Weapons during the 1991 Persian Gulf War." *The Nonproliferation Review* (Spring–Summer 1997).

Turkay, Selen. "Setting Goals: Who, Why, How." Harvard Office of the Vice Provost for Advances in Learning, 2014.

Walker, Sam. *The Captain Class.* New York: Penguin, 2017.

Wiley, Carolyn. "What Motivates Employees According to Over 40 Years of Motivation Surveys." *International Journal of Manpower* 18 (1997): 263–80.

Willink, Joclo, and Leif Babin. *Extreme Ownership.* New York: St. Martin's Press, 2015.

Xenophon. *Cyropaedia (Education by Cyrus).* Translated by Walter Miller. Cambridge, MA: Harvard University Press, Loeb Classical Library, 1914.

Zak, Paul. "The Neuroscience of Trust." *Harvard Business Review* (January–February 2017).

Zak, Paul. *Trust Factor.* New York: American Management Association, 2017.

Zhang, Haiyan. "How Do I Recognize Thee, Let Me Count the Ways." Thought Leadership Whitepaper, IBM Smarter Workforce Institute, 2015.

INDEX

absenteeism, team culture and, 30
Afghanistan, 24, 25, 26–28
Alexander the Great, 3
Allen, Commander, 127–31
American Revolution, 168, 169–70
Ancell, Manning R., 172, 191
anger, 173
approachability, 14, 84–88, 170; pitfalls
    of, 85–88
Aristide, Jean-Bertrand, 205n2
Aristotle, 3
arrogance, 109–10, 186
asynchronous webinars, 171
Atkinson, Rick, 152–53
attrition, bad leaders and, 24–25, 26, 45
authenticity, 57, 171–72
Axelrod, Alan, 144

bad leaders: and attrition, 24–25, 26, 45;
    bad news and, 95–100; characteristics
    of, 25; and crisis, 167–68; impact of,
    25–27, 45–46; and interactions,
    39–41

bad news: bad leaders and, 95–100; good
    leaders and, 100–101; on
    performance, 118
barriers, physical, removing, 58, 60, 122,
    126
battle glasses, 51, 198n21
behaviors of caring leadership, 4,
    177–78; barriers to, 163–64;
    combining, importance of, 19–20;
    getting to know you, 55–74;
    optimism, 137–62; recognition,
    113–36; respect, 93–111; study of,
    29; visibility, 75–92
Bible. See Holy Bible
biological weapons, 48
Blanchard, Kenneth, 191
Blankenship, Charles, 171
board of directors: speaking mind in,
    83–84; recognition and, 115–16
Bodenheimer, George, 185–86
body language, 41, 45, 83, 122, 143
Bonaparte, Napoleon, 137, 151
Borneman, Walter, 189

Bossidy, Larry, 55
Brouker, Jake, 13–14
Brouker, Kris, 12, 49, 52, 98
Brouker, Paul, 7–8, 9f
Brouker, Steve, 9–10
Brouker Leadership Solutions, 1
Buckingham, Marcus, 186
Burchell, Michael, 190
Bureau of Naval Personnel, 23–24,
    195n1

calmness, 94; in crisis, 172–73, 174, 175;
    and performance correction, 122
Capparell, Stephanie, 138, 189
Captain's Calls, 171
Captain's Masts, 158, 165, 204n16
caring leadership: first meeting and,
    57–58; history of, 3; impact of,
    90–91; importance of, 2, 10, 12;
    insights on, 7–21; models of, 8;
    opportunities for, 37–53; prioritizing,
    1–2. *See also* behaviors of caring lead-
    ership
Carnegie, Dale, 187
cascade effect, 31
cell phones, 199n23
challenges: leadership quality and,
    99–100; optimism and, 145. *See also*
    crisis leadership
Charan, Ram, 55
chemical weapons, 48, 51, 198n22
chief petty officers (chiefs), 86, 193n1;
    importance of, 9–10; Smock, 11–12;
    Tandy, 8, 9f
chief's mess, 65, 124, 200n7
Churchill, Winston, 144–45
circle of influence, 145–50
civic action program, 45, 197n13
civility. *See* respect
Coffman, Curt, 186

Cofield, Barry, 37–38
cognition: exercise and, 158–59; inci-
    vility and, 104–5
Collins, Jim, 144, 186
colonoscopy screenings, 129–30, 203n5
Comfort, USNS, 47–52, 171, 197n8,
    199n24
command and control, leadership by, 25,
    167. *See also* bad leaders
Command Ashore insignia, 201n4
command climate surveys, 15, 16, 77,
    194n8
commanding officers (COs), 12, 87,
    194n3
Command Leadership School, 55–58
command pin. *See* Command Ashore
    insignia
command sergeant major (CSM), 40,
    196n3
communication channels, for recog-
    nition, 114
communications: deployment and,
    51–52, 199n23; with family, 154–55
compassion, 1, 3, 177. *See also* caring
    leadership
competency, 2
connecting the dots, 44–45; examples
    of, 43–44; importance of, 47;
    optimism and, 160; walking around
    and, 89
consistency, 2
contagion, social, 31–32, 34
Continental Army, 168, 169–70
control: and behavior change, 164–65,
    178; circle of influence and, 145–46;
    and crisis, 174; leaders and, 14
coronavirus crisis, 168–69
corporate environment, 17, 31; and
    circle of influence, 148–50; and

pessimism, 139–40; and showing care, 65–66
cortisol, 102
COs. *See* commanding officers
counterinsurgency, 44, 197n12
Countryman, Tom, 124
Covey, Stephen, 128, 145–46, 185
Crawford, Master Chief, 65, 90
creases, military, 199n1
creativity, team culture and, 30
credibility, 171
crisis leadership, 167–75; key points on, 175; and respect, 94–95; and visibility, 91
CSM. *See* command sergeant major
culture. *See* fear, culture of; team culture; trust, culture of
customer service, leadership and, 31–32

decision making: prayer and, 159; walking around and, 82
Deeter, Commander, 49–50, 198n17
Delmo, Charity, 155–56
dental readiness, 15, 194n5
Department Organization Climate Survey, 15, 16, 77, 194n8
detailers, 23–24
difficult conversations, 122–25; recommendations for, 126
discipline: and behavior change, 164, 165; and getting-to-know-you meetings, 59–60
disengagement, term, 17
disrespect. *See* incivility
Dominguez, Frank, 116–17
dopamine, 159

efficiency, limits of, 121–22
effort, tolerating poor performance and, 119–20

Einstein, Albert, 163
Eisenhower, Dwight, 152–53
emotional intelligence, 188
emotional reactions, allowing time for, 122
emulation of leader, 33; and customer service, 31–32; and work-life balance, 155
Endurance, 137–38, 138f
engagement: emulation and, 31; and performance, 30; recognition and, 114; term, 17; work-life balance and, 156
ensigns, 11, 194n2
EvergreenHealth Medical Center, 168
executive coaching, 16–17
executive officers (XOs), 60–61, 199n2
exercise, 153, 157–59
extroverts, and visibility, 85

Faison, Forrest, 100–101, 133
faith. *See* prayer
faking optimism, 152–53
family: reintegration, 41, 196n5; and Shanahan and, 38; time for, 153–56; workplace stress and, 102. *See also* work-life balance
family physicians, training and qualifications of, 195n11–12
favoritism, 45; avoiding appearance of, 83
fear, culture of, 13, 14, 45–46; and crisis, 173; effects of, 95–100, 102–5
first meeting(s), 55–74; examples of, 61–65; key points on, 73; old approach to, 61
Fisher, Wink, 52, 53
fitness reports, 25, 195n2
flexibility, with time, 121–22, 123, 129
force protection, 15, 195n10

Fortune 100 Best Companies to Work For, 29–30
Fortune 500, and work-life balance, 156
Fox, HM3, 42–44
Fox, Jeffrey, 186–87
Frankl, Viktor, 4

Gallup, 31, 186
getting-to-know-you meetings, 55–74, 170; essentials of, 60; key points on, 73–74; and visibility, 88, 90–91
goals: in getting-to-know-you meeting, 67; setting, 67–68; for training, 133
Goldsmith, Marshall, 167
Goleman, Daniel, 188
good leaders: bad news and, 100–101; influence of, 17–18, 43–45, 52–53; and retention, 24–25
government shutdown, 75–78, 201n1
Great Place to Work (GPTW) Institute, 29–30, 190

Haiti, 205n2
Hanoi Hilton, 144, 203n2
Harvard Business Review, 164
HM3, 197n10. *See also* Fox, HM3; Lent, HM3
Hỏa Lò Prison. *See* Hanoi Hilton
Holy Bible, 190–91
honesty, in crisis, 172, 174
hope: Churchill and, 144; in crisis, 174; Napoleon and, 137, 151
Houser, Kurt, 72, 124
humility, 142–43, 186; emulation of, 31–32; team culture and, 43
Hussein, Saddam, 48, 50, 51, 198n22

IBM Smarter Workforce Institute, 114, 117
Ideal Visa Consultancy, 155–56

incivility: effects of, 102–5; as performance issue, 120–22, 123, 132–33
Individual Augmentee, 41, 196n4
informal visits. *See* walking around
information: in crisis, 170–71; informal conversations and, 79–80, 84; and morale, 50–52; updating, 75–78
Integrated Disability Evaluation System, 15, 194n9
interactions, 37–53, 178; key points on, 53; and poor performance, 120; respecting time in, 57–58, 68–69, 105–7, 108–9; walking around and, 82
internet, 199n23
intimidation, 13–14, 45; commanding officers and, 87; XOs and, 61
introverts, and visibility, 85
Iraq, 24, 25, 27–28, 42–44, 47–52
Islam, 43–44, 197n11
Iverson, Ken, 75–76, 77, 78, 201n2

Johnson, Spencer, 191
Joint Commission Accreditation, 95, 201n2
Jones, Bert, 190–91
Jones, Lieutenant, 63–65

Kearns Goodwin, Doris, 93
Keegan, John, 75
key points: on continuous learning, 165; on crisis leadership, 175; on interactions, 53; on leadership, 21, 35; on optimism, 161–62; on recognition, 135–36; on respect, 110–11; on visibility, 91–92
King, Commander, 125–27, 130
King, Lieutenant, 96–98

Kolenda, Christopher, 7, 187–88
Kuwait, 47–48, 50

labor issues, 70–72
leaders: dominating conversation,
57–58, 68–69, 105, 106–7; influence
of, 17–18, 23, 28, 41–53, 90–91,
142, 170; and intimidation, 13–14,
87; scrutiny of, 39, 119. *See also* bad
leaders; good leaders
leadership: continuous learning on,
163–65; and customer service,
31–32; insights on, 7–21; key points
on, 21, 35; as phenomenon, 23,
34–35; power of, 23–35; study of,
13, 17, 27–30
leadership lessons: on attrition, 26; on
awareness versus ownership, 66; on
bad news, 101; on behaviors, 19; on
caring, 12; on connecting the dots,
47; on continuous learning, 164; on
crisis, 95, 171, 173; on difficult
conversations, 126; on disrespect,
105; on effects of ignoring poor
performance, 119, 120; on
emulation, 33; on fit with job, 134;
on flexibility, 123; on getting-to-
know-you meetings, 60, 70; on goal
questions, 68; on interactions, 39; on
mentoring, 109; on optimism, 139,
146; on pessimism, 140, 141, 152; on
power of leadership, 32; on proactive
approaches, 168; on recognition,
115, 118; on reducing intimidation,
14; on respect, 94; on seeking understanding, 132; on team culture, 34;
on time respect, 107; on trust, 20; on
visibility, 79, 82, 89; on work-life
balance, 160

leadership philosophy, 12; and
performance, 15–16
learning, continuous, 163–65; importance of, 163; key point on, 165
Lent, HM3, 45–46
limited duty program, 15, 194n6
Lincoln, Abraham, 3–4, 93
listening: and caring leadership, 59; in
difficult conversations, 126; empathetic, 128; in getting-to-know-you
meetings, 58, 69; and respect,
109–10
love: and resilience, 27; term, 4. *See also*
caring leadership

mail, 51–52, 199n23
Marshall, George, 152
master chiefs, 65–66, 86, 90, 200n3
Maxwell, John C., 190
mental health advisory teams (MHATs),
27–28
mentoring, 85; versus micromanaging,
108–9; recommendations for, 109
Mercy, USNS, 42, 45–46, 197n8
micromanaging, 25, 26–27, 45, 107–8;
versus mentoring, 108–9
mindfulness, and work-life balance, 153
Mission Oriented Protective Posture
(MOPP), 51, 52
morale: Persian Gulf War and, 50–52;
pessimism and, 147; Shackleton and,
137–38; work-life balance and, 155
Morrell, Margot, 138, 189
Mortuary Affairs, 41–44, 197n6
multitasking: as arrogance, 109–10;
avoiding, 60

Naval Hospital Bethesda, 47
Naval Hospital Bremerton, 15–16,
70–72, 78–80, 194n4, 195n11,

201n2; colonoscopy screenings, 129–30; Patient Centered Medical Home, 80–82

Naval Hospital San Diego, 10

Naval War College, 13

Navy Medical Inspector General Program, 95, 201n3

Navy Medicine West, 15–16, 68

necrotizing enterocolitis (NEC), 103–4, 202n15

neurotransmitters: exercise and, 159; leadership quality and, 102

Nimitz, Chester, 189

non-commissioned officers (NCOs), 2, 64–65, 124, 193n1

nonjudicial punishment proceedings. *See* Captain's Masts

noradrenaline, 159

officer of the day (OOD), 108, 202n18

Operation Desert Shield/Storm, 47–52

Operation Unified Endeavour, 197n9

Operation Uphold Democracy, 171, 204n2

opportunities, 178; crisis and, 95, 174–75; interactions as, 37–53

optimism, 137–62; in crisis, 172, 173–74, 75; exercise and, 158–59; faking, 152–53; key points on, 161–62; practice of, 143–50, 152–53; resources on, 192

ownership: of issues, versus awareness, 66; of team culture, 33–34

oxytocin, 102

Pacific Partnership 2008, 42, 197n9

pay disparities, addressing, 147–48

Peale, Norman Vincent, 113, 192

performance: culture of fear and, 102–3; feedback on, 113–36; goal setting and, 68; leadership philosophy and, 15–16; mild incivility and, 103–5; team culture and, 29–32, 33–34; trust and, 30, 169; work-life balance and, 156–57

Persian Gulf War, 47–52

pessimism, 139–43; effects of, 140–41, 151–52; resisting, 142–43

phenomenon: definition of, 23; leadership as, 23, 34–35

Plato, 3

POMI officer, 198n17

poor performance: confronting, 120–30; ignoring, 118–20; persistent, 132–33; roots of, 125–30

Porath, Christine, 188

posttraumatic stress disorder (PTSD), 41; leadership quality and, 28; Mortuary Affairs and, 42

Powell, Colin, 59

practice, for performance correction, 122–23

praise, 113–18; list, 115–16

prayer, 153, 159

preparation: for crisis, 167; for performance correction, 122–23

prescription cost control team, 141–43

presence, 75–92

private sector. *See* corporate environment

proactive approaches, 168–69; to getting to know you, 59; to recognition, 116; to walking around, 83

problem areas, identification of, 78

PTSD. *See* posttraumatic stress disorder

questions: for first meeting, 58; making time for, 76–77

realism: in crisis, 174; and optimism, 143–45

recognition, 113–36; barriers to, 117; key points on, 135–36; walking around and, 89

reintegration, 41, 196n5

relationship building, 16–17, 177; as low priority, 18–19; resources on, 187; and team culture, 30

resilience, leadership quality and, 27–28

respect, 93–111; importance of, 93; key points on, 110–11

retention, 24; family-friendly policies and, 157; good leaders and, 24–25; recognition and, 114

Revolutionary War, 168, 169–70

Robin, Jennifer, 190

Roosevelt, Theodore, 1, 4

rudeness. *See* incivility

Sandberg, Sheryl, 171

scheduling. *See* time

Scott, Kim, 170

SCUD missiles, 51, 198n20

serotonin, 159

Sexton, Dan, 42

Shackleton, Ernest, 137–38, 189

Shanahan, Mike, 37–38

Smock, Chief, 11–12

social events, objective for, 83

social media platforms, for recognition, 114

sports: and leadership, 185–86, 189–90; and trust building, 37–38

staff, getting to know, 55–74

stakeholders, getting-to-know-you meetings with, 58

Stavridis, James, 172, 191

Stevens, David, 190–91

Stockdale, James, 144, 174

Stockdale Paradox, 144

story, in getting-to-know-you meeting, 57–58

synchronous webinars, 171

Tandy, Chief, 8, 9f

team, getting to know, 55–74

team culture: nature of, 32–33; ownership of, 33–34; and performance, 29–32, 33–34; respect and, 93–94, 101–5; volatility of, 142

termination, 118, 133, 134, 148

Third Party Collection Program, 194n7

time: flexibility with, 121–22, 123, 129; for getting-to-know-you meetings, 59–60, 69–70, 72–73; for performance correction, 121–23, 125; for recognition, 116–17; of subordinates, respecting, 57–58, 68–69, 105–7, 108–9. *See also* work-life balance

training, 133, 134

transfer, 133, 134

transparency, and getting-to-know-you meetings, 69

trauma: bad leadership and, 25–27; leadership quality and, 27–28

trust, 2, 7, 135; assessment of, 77; culture of, 16, 101–2, 169; versus disrespect, 108; importance of, 19–20, 178; interactions and, 37–53; as low priority, 18; and performance, 30, 169; seeking understanding and, 131; Smock on, 12; tolerating poor performance and, 119–20

truth: versus coverup, 98; in crisis, 170–71; trust and, 78–80 turnover: family-friendly policies and, 157; team culture and, 30

understanding, seeking, 127–31; barriers to, 131; frequency of, 131–32; value of, 130–31

visibility, 75–92, 170; and approachability, 84–88; key points on, 91–92; and knowing your staff, 88, 90–91; optimizing, 92; pitfalls of, 85–88
vulnerability, 57; and getting-to-know-you meetings, 69

Walker, Sam, 189–90
walking around, 75–92, 168–70; examples of, 78–83; key points on, 91–92; and knowing your staff, 88, 90–91; optimizing, 92; pitfalls of, 83, 89, 92; and recognition, 116–17; recommendations for, 89, 92
Walter Reed National Military Medical Center, 150
webinars, 171
"Why Am I Talking" (WAIT), 106, 107
Williams, Lieutenant Commander, 66–67
working memory, incivility and, 104–5
work-life balance, 153–60, 185; limits of, 121; respect for time and, 105–6

Xenophon, 3
XOs. *See* executive officers

ABOUT THE AUTHOR

.**Captain Mark Brouker**, United States Navy (Retired), is a thought leader, sought-after keynote speaker, professor, historian, executive coach, and author. Recipient of numerous military and civilian leadership awards, he has served in an array of leadership positions, including fifteen years in the C-suite during and after his thirty-year Navy career. Captain Brouker served as commanding officer at one of the largest naval hospitals in the world. He also served as chief of staff for Navy Medicine West, responsible for ten hospitals spanning the West Coast to the Indian Ocean and health care for eight hundred thousand patients. In this position, he provided executive coaching for ten commanding officers.

After transitioning from the military, Dr. Brouker founded Brouker Leadership Solutions, a company passionate about helping leaders succeed on their leadership journey. Dr. Brouker has presented to thousands of professionals from diverse organizations in twenty-one countries on five continents, including an array of Fortune 500 companies, professional and military organizations, and top universities. His podcasts and blogs, as well as his TED talk, can be found at his company website, www.broukerleadershipsolutions.com.

Captain Brouker volunteers as an executive coach at the Honor Foundation, a nonprofit organization that helps U.S. Navy SEALs and other Special Operations Forces military personnel transition from the military environment to the corporate environment.

Captain Brouker lives in San Diego, California, with his wife, Kris. Married in 1983, they have three children—Shayna, Jake, and Katherine—and one grandchild, Jonah, son of Shayna and their son-in-law Joe.